Let's CLEAR the AIR

With a
Foreword by:
Christy Turlington

REASONS NOT TO START SMOKING

Lobster Press™

Published by Lobster Press™
1620 Sherbrooke Street West, Suites C & D
Montréal, Québec   H3H 1C9
Tel. (514) 904-1100 • Fax (514) 904-1101 • www.lobsterpress.com

Publisher: Alison Fripp
Editors: Alison Fripp & Meghan Nolan
Head Writer: Faye Smailes
Contributors: Lauren Clark, Alison Kilian, Nisa Raizen-Miller
Indexer: Estalita Slivoskey
Book Designer: Patrick Franc
Production Manager: Tammy Desnoyers

The essays in this book were submitted as original work, and in some cases, were edited for clarity. The statements, opinions, views, and comments reflect the views of the independent contributors and not those of Lobster Press.

Library and Archives Canada Cataloguing in Publication

Let's clear the air: 10 reasons not to start smoking

ISBN 978-1-897073-66-7

1. Smoking--Prevention--Juvenile literature.

HV5745.L48 2007   j613.85   C2007-901573-5

Printed and bound in Canada.

CONTENTS

FOREWORD

by Christy Turlington

I remember when I first started smoking. I was thirteen. My dad had always smoked and like so many other kids who later become smokers, I hated it. By the time I started junior high school, my older sister and her friends began to smoke. And by the time I started high school, my friends and I were smoking as well. I can't really pinpoint when or why I picked up that first cigarette, or at what point my feelings about cigarettes and smoking went from disgust to intrigue, but I did know that it didn't take long for me to become a "smoker." This was also around the time that I started to model. And though my mother usually accompanied me to appointments, believe me I took every chance I could when she wasn't around to light up a cigarette. I was always surrounded by people who smoked – photographers, celebrities, models – and who made it look like the thing to do. With a cigarette between my fingers, I felt like I always had something to do. I thought it made me look sophisticated.

I began my long battle to quit smoking at the age of nineteen, when I first admitted to myself that I was addicted to cigarettes. I finally quit at the age of 26. I had no idea it would be so hard. At first I tried every known cessation method out there. Eventually I got fed up and I gave up smoking for good, quitting cold turkey. I was embarrassed by all the failed attempts. I could no longer look at myself in the mirror after so many false promises of taking better care of myself. My dad had a different story. Despite having a heart attack at the age of fifty and going through angioplasty, he resumed smoking. In fairness, he did try to quit several times as well but it was only when he began coughing up blood a dozen years later that he was finally able to quit for good. I had always pleaded with my dad to quit, especially after I had, showing him I was proof he could do it. Sadly, he was diagnosed with lung cancer just weeks after quitting. He died six months later in June 1997. He was 64 years old and had smoked for over 50 years. The one thing I was most thankful for during my dad's illness was that I wasn't still smoking. Another was that he didn't have to endure lung cancer for any longer than he did. This is when I began to understand the importance of prevention rather than just focusing on quitting.

Looking back I realize that I had wanted to emulate my father's behavior and then later being young and a model in the fashion industry in which so many people smoke, I had put a lot of pressure on myself to "fit in." Smoking made me think I was a rebel when I was really just following others. What I realize now is that the truly rebellious thing to have done then would have been never to have started. When I was approached to write the foreword for this book, I found myself awed by the brave essays written by youths encouraging peers not to start, encouraging relatives to quit, and proudly proclaiming themselves as smoke-free. Reading their words and remembering how difficult it was for me to quit smoking, I only wish I'd had a book like this before I ever tried it. This book, these essays, the reasons inside – this is what makes a true rebel. To you, its readers, I encourage you to support each other, to continue to educate others, and to take the pledge at the end of the book, along with family and friends, to stay smoke-free. After all, your life depends on it.

© 2007 CHRISTY TURLINGTON

INTRODUCTION

Everyone's talking about quitting smoking, but as we learn more about the sickness and death that cigarette butts leave in their wake, what we don't understand is why anyone would start smoking in the first place. It's time to cut to the chase and clear the air for good.

We've asked over forty kids to tell us why they don't smoke and why they never will. For them, it's not about quitting smoking. It's about remaining smoke-free and in control of their bodies and their lives. Many of the kids submitted personal essays and statements in an effort to make their reasons for not smoking crystal clear (the ✍ symbol throughout the book marks their own words). What they talk and write about is real, raw, thought-provoking, and even controversial. You'll hear from Adrienne, who lost her dad to lung cancer caused by smoking, and Adam, whose father suffered a stroke as a result of his cigarette habit but still smokes. You'll hear from kids like Margaret, who feel that smokers aren't fun friends or attractive boyfriends and girlfriends, and Justin, who took a chance and started a petition in his home state to ban people from smoking in their cars when young children are present. Each of these kids has a special story and unique view to share, but one main message connects them all: smoking is NOT for them and it never will be. They don't think anyone should start the habit, and they're not afraid to tell you why.

When asked, the kids' main motivation for not smoking is to avoid its deadly effects. They also offer nine additional reasons why we should all be smoke-free, just in case dying isn't reason enough, or in case there is anyone who still might believe that if they take up smoking, they won't get sick.

This book is divided into ten chapters according to the ten reasons not to start smoking. You can read the chapters out of order and skip to the reasons that interest or surprise you most. Along the way, you'll come across sidebars that will let you in on some of the disturbing and lesser-known facts that tobacco companies hope you'll never learn. You'll also see some of the graphic warnings that smokers look at every time they pick up their packs of cigarettes. Toward the end (pp. 189-191), you'll find definitions for the words in bold within the book, as well as a list of resources. When you're done reading, see page 180, which explains how you too can start taking action against tobacco by making a written pledge to be smoke-free always. Join the ranks of kids who want it to be known all around the world that choosing *not* to start smoking in the first place is the only decision. And then keep up the fight. Don't give anyone a reason to call you a quitter.

CANCER + OTHER
SMOKING-RELATED ILLNESSES

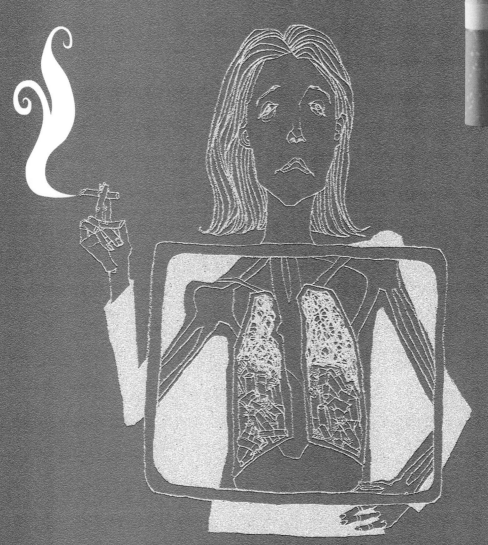

Adrienne Joy Lowry, 12

Adrienne has come face-to-face with the dangers of smoking. She was only seven when her father, a smoker, died of cancer. Adrienne's dad may have smoked, but she won't. She has too many reasons not to – Adrienne knows a lot of people who have lost loved ones because of smoking. Even though she misses her dad very much, Adrienne hasn't let what smoking has done to her family ruin her life. She loves sports, books, Harry Potter movies, and her Nintendo DS, and she says that she's lucky to have a good role model in her big sister, Mackenzie (age 18), who doesn't smoke and has worked in tobacco control programs since she was 14.

INSTANT HISTORY FACTS

People haven't always known that cigarettes kill. In 1964, the United States released the first study by a government that linked smoking to **lung cancer, heart disease**, and **emphysema**.[1]

Now we know that cigarette smoking is the cause of many other diseases, such as **leukemia, cataracts, pneumonia, strokes**, and cancers of the cervix, kidney, pancreas, and stomach. The chemicals from cigarettes go everywhere that blood flows, so smoking causes diseases in nearly every organ of the body.[2]

Adrienne thinks that spreading the word about how harmful cigarettes are will help to keep people from ever starting the habit in the first place. She knows that by telling her story, she is helping others.

In Adrienne's own words...

My Dad and Smoking

"Where's Daddy," I asked. I knew it was a weekend so he would be home. I had just come back from a sleepover at my friend Sierra's house. My mom's face was red as she said, "Daddy went to the hospital last night because he wasn't feeling very good. It will be all right." I didn't really understand, but I knew something was wrong. I went upstairs to get Bobo, my stuffed cat. Then the phone rang. A few minutes later, my mommy told me that we were going to go to the hospital to see Daddy. I got into the car with Bobo and we drove to the hospital with the "oldies" playing. When we got there, the doctor came in and told my mom that Dad was going to have to go to a hospital in another state – Minnesota.

Later we went to the hospital in Minnesota and saw Daddy. He was attached to all of these wires and had a big air tank by his bed. He didn't look very good. The doctor came in and said that he would need to be scanned for cancer and it would take a few hours. That night my mom took me and my sister, Mackenzie, to my aunt's house. We stayed there for about a week. Then we went to my stepsister Eileen's house. She has horses. I rode a horse named Rosie. It was the first horse I had ever ridden. After a week and a half there, I went back to my aunt's in Wisconsin. We went to the hospital every day to be with my daddy. The doctor told my mom that he did not have cancer and that he could go home soon. When we did go home, my sister had to give him three shots every day. After missing two months of second grade, I came back to find my best friend, Stephanie, waiting for me at the school doors. When I got to Mrs. Quintus's class there was an envelope with my name on it. Mrs. Quintus gave me the envelope and inside there were cards to me and my family from my classmates. That put a huge smile on my face. When I showed all the cards to my dad later on he had a huge smile on his face too.

The next day I went to school and when I came home, the hospital bed was gone and I asked "Where's Daddy?" My mom said that he went back to the hospital because he was getting worse. We went to the hospital and he had a deck of cards on his bed. He was going to teach me how to play solitaire. Then three doctors came in and said that he *did* have cancer, but it was so deep in his lungs that they did not see it coming the first time they scanned for cancer. He had heart and lung cancer. He got it from smoking, they said, and that it was getting worse and he probably wasn't going to make it. Right that very second I started to cry. I remember that room. Most of our family was in there. After that, I realized how serious this was.

Two weeks later I went trick-or-treating. I was a black cat and so was my sister, Mackenzie. My dad was in hospice. I brought him some of my leftover candy. He didn't eat it though. The doctors didn't want him to. I made Daddy a little green ring out of pipe cleaner. Little did I know that was my last day with him.

My dad died on November 2, 2002. I wrote this in my

journal on the day that he died:

Today my daddy died. It was really sad. I will miss him. He took his last breath and then poof he was gone. His spirit went to heaven. He is special.

On November 9, 2002 I went to my daddy's funeral. I wrote a poem and read it to everyone. It went like this: *The wind blew while the sun grew. And then it happened. It was sad, everyone cried. I cried but it didn't help because there was nothing I could do.*

My dad, Jack Lowry, died when I was seven years old and now I am twelve. All of the memories of my dad are crystal clear. I really miss him. He was a great daddy!

I wish my dad had never started smoking because then he would not have died from lung cancer. I will never smoke because I don't want my kids someday to have to go through what I went through.

DID YOU KNOW?

There weren't always warning labels on cigarette packages. In 1965, the United States was the first country to require a warning on all of the cigarette packs sold in the country. The warning stated: "Caution – cigarette smoking may be hazardous to your health."[3]

In 2000, Canada was the first to require that health labels with color pictures be printed on cigarette packages. The warnings include pictures of a diseased mouth, a lung **tumor**, a brain after a **stroke**, a damaged heart, and a limp cigarette as a warning about **impotence** (look for the symbol throughout the book for examples of some of the images that Canada prints on cigarette packs).[4] Canada's cigarette packages were even displayed in New York's Museum of Modern Art in 2005 as part of an exhibition of designs from around the world that aim to protect the mind and body from danger.[5]

Other countries also use or plan to use picture-based health warnings, including Australia[6], Belgium[7], Brazil[8], Chile[9], Jordan[10], New Zealand[11], Singapore[12], Switzerland[13], Thailand[14], and Venezuela.[15, 16]

Cigarette packages sold in the United States today still only have four sentences total in their list of warnings[17] – that's less information on a cigarette package than there is on a chocolate bar![18] As a result of the Comprehensive Smoking Education Act passed by Congress in 1984, a rotation of four black-and-white, short text warnings on cigarette packages was introduced. Since then, the U.S. cigarette pack warnings have alerted people to such dangers as **cancer**, **heart disease**, and **emphysema**, as well as to the fact that cigarette smoke contains **carbon monoxide**[19].

These images were required to be placed on Australian retail packages of tobacco under Australian legislation passed in August 2004. The images also appear on cigarette packages in Canada.

Aanchal Chugh, 11

Aanchal is thankful for the positive, smoke-free role models in her life. Her mother, an echocardiographer (someone who conducts special tests to evaluate people's hearts) gets a first-hand look at the damage that cigarettes cause to the hearts of smokers. Aanchal's older brother, Ankur (16), is an anti-smoking activist, speaking out against tobacco on behalf of the American Heart Association. One of the reasons Aanchal, like her brother, is concerned about smoking's effects is because her grandmother, a nonsmoker, got tongue cancer as a result of being exposed to secondhand smoke. Her grandmother can no longer taste anything – because of the cancer, she has lost all of her taste buds.

> ## FAST FACTS
>
> Smoking has serious effects on the body right away. Besides the immediate bad breath, irritated eyes and throat, and increased heartbeat and blood pressure, young smokers also have **respiratory** problems, reduced **immunity** against illnesses, tooth decay and tooth loss, gum disease, chronic coughing, increased headaches, and increased stress. Kids and teens who smoke can also experience hearing loss, and because smoke smells so much, smokers actually lose some of their sense of smell.[20]

Aanchal hates the smell of smoke, and knows that if it were her, she would feel bad if *she* were making others-around her sick. She believes that secondhand smoke is something that nonsmokers, like her and her grandmother, shouldn't have to deal with. Aanchal worries that the younger kids at her middle school might be influenced to smoke by the older students they look up to, and thinks that tougher laws should be put in place to keep kids from cigarettes. She specifies that she has much better things to do than smoke – she enjoys reading books from the *Series of Unfortunate Events*, writing, swimming, and playing with her pet rabbit, Angel. Aanchal hopes that her words will inspire people everywhere not to smoke.

 In Aanchal's own words ...

What Does Smoking Do to Your Body?

If I were granted one wish, it would be to make all cigarette companies stop selling cigarettes. If cigarette companies stopped selling cigarettes, then people wouldn't be able to *start* smoking and people would also have to *stop* smoking. Most kids start smoking because they think it's cool and they want to be part of the group. When they realize the mistake they have made, it's too late because now they can't stop.

There is not one good reason to start smoking, but there are several bad reasons. So many people die every year because of smoking. Smoking causes lung cancer, breast cancer, tongue cancer, and throat cancer. Cancer doesn't only kill you – it can destroy the quality of your life when you're living. When people smoke, their fingernails and teeth turn yellow, their breath smells horrible, and they get wrinkles faster.

So many people die every day because of heart disease. Although there are different causes of heart disease, smoking is one of the major reasons. Smoking clogs arteries and makes them narrower. When arteries get narrower, they cannot supply enough blood to the heart, and the heart has trouble beating. The heart is one of the most important organs in our bodies. Don't you think we should not smoke so we can take good care of our hearts? Smoking also causes lung cancer and other breathing-related diseases. Lungs are the main body part that helps us breath. People who smoke carry dirty air in their lungs. This dirty air, over a period of time, stops the proper functioning of the lungs.

ACTIVIST MOMENTS

Even though the U.S. government has recognized the danger of smoking since the 1960s, **tobacco companies** denied this fact until 1997![21] Lowell Bergman, a reporter for the TV program *60 Minutes*, fought to air an interview with a scientist who told people the truth: that tobacco companies had long known the harmful effects of smoking. Tobacco companies threatened to sue the TV station, but the interview was finally shown in 1996 anyway, and soon after, a big tobacco company admitted for the first time that smoking is **addictive** and causes **cancer**.[22] Lowell Bergman's story was made into a movie called *The Insider* (1999), which was nominated for seven Oscars.

FAST FACTS

*When someone smokes a cigarette, he or she inhales over 4,000 chemicals.[23] The toxic, poisonous mix of substances includes ingredients also found in chemical weapons, batteries, paint stripper, the bleach in toilet cleaners, nail polish remover, car exhaust, and rat poison.[24] Cigarettes also contain a sticky black tar made up of thousands of chemicals that stays in the smoker's lungs and causes **cancer**.[25]*

Phillip Oravec, 11

When Phillip grows up, he wants to be an architect and design buildings like the Notre Dame Cathedral. He loves drawing blueprints and always gets As or Bs in art class. When Phillip thinks about cigarettes, he imagines how smoking would affect his favorite thing to do. "If my art isn't good, it must be my attitude. I've heard that drugs can mess your attitude up. I may forget what I'm drawing or think something isn't what it is when I draw it. By not taking any type of drugs,

FAST FACTS

Most cigarettes have **filters**, which are dotted with tiny holes to let more air through and less smoke. The problem with filters is that smokers will just smoke more to get the dose of nicotine that their bodies want, so the same amount of chemicals will end up being inhaled. Filtered cigarettes are not lighter or safer. Light cigarettes do not reduce the health risks of smoking.[26]

including **nicotine**, I know what's happening. I'll be healthy, aware, and I won't lose my brain cells."

He has heard statistics that suggest that for every cigarette you smoke, seven minutes are cut off your life. He's done the math and points out that this equals 140 minutes gone from your life for every pack smoked. If a friend offered him a cigarette, Phillip would tell them that they aren't his friend if they want him to smoke. "Smoking may seem cool, but it's not. Unless you think death is cool."

Phillip has seen pictures of smokers' hearts and lungs, shriveled and black from nicotine and tar. "It's like their organs have been inside a mummy for years," he says. He thinks that companies shouldn't be allowed to invent drugs that give you upper-respiratory problems and ruin the type of alertness he'll need to be an architect. "It's devastating how they do this stupid stuff that messes with your mind. If I smoked, I could be too sick to draw at all."

Phillip's personal reasons for not starting to smoke are clear – his mental and physical health are too important. He offers his thoughts below on why no one should ever start the habit.

 In Phillip's own words ...

Smoking can cause lung, heart and brain cancer and other diseases. No matter how tempting it is to start smoking, it is even harder to quit. Just because a friend, brother or sister or parents and celebrities smoke, doesn't mean you should too. Hundreds of thousands of people die from smoking and many – tens of thousands of people – die from breathing the smoke every year.

One pack of cigarettes costs about $5.00 (in the United States). Companies want you to buy the cigarettes, because they don't care if you die or get sick. They just want the money. Smoking is not cool because it kills. The factories are putting more of a drug called nicotine into each cigarette. Nicotine is a drug – when you take it, your body has to have more of it. So, when there is more nicotine put in a cigarette, you have to have more and more, so you have to always buy more cigarettes.

I wish our town had a no smoking ban like our school has. There are more restaurants that won't let people smoke. We go to these places because we don't have to smell the cigarette smoke. I wish the whole world would just stop smoking.

Cigarettes are a waste of your money, but there is a bigger waste: of your life! Don't ever start to smoke.

SMOKING STATS

Every 6.5 seconds, someone in the world dies from a disease caused by smoking.[27]

The typical smoker will die 13 to 14 years earlier than a nonsmoker.[28]

500 million people who are alive today will eventually be killed by tobacco.[29]

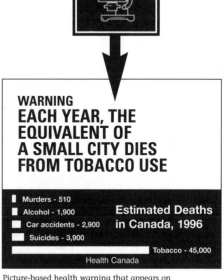

WARNING
EACH YEAR, THE EQUIVALENT OF A SMALL CITY DIES FROM TOBACCO USE

■ Murders - 510	**Estimated Deaths in Canada, 1996**
■ Alcohol - 1,900	
■ Car accidents - 2,900	
■ Suicides - 3,900	
Tobacco - 45,000	

Health Canada

Picture-based health warning that appears on cigarette packages in Canada.
Licensed under Health Canada copyright.

RELATIONSHIPS AND PEER PRESSURE

Margaret Caruso, 12

Like all of us, Margaret Caruso has her own thoughts about what is "cool." For Margaret, being cool and having fun means watching *American Idol* and game shows on TV; it's dancing around to her favorite music; or simply hanging out with her friends. She thinks that the farthest thing from having fun – and the least likely way to win lots of friends and admirers – would be to start smoking. "People are not attracted to you when you have yellow teeth and, like, really bad breath," she explains. Even just by looking at the way smoking is used in the movies, Margaret can't imagine how cigarettes could ever be associated with being hip. "When you see people smoking in movies, they're usually drunk, or they usually have, like, a problem or something," she observes. "It's as if most of the time, they're usually the bad character in the movie."

Having lived in New York City all of her life, Margaret finds that it's hard enough to have to deal with the fumes of buses and cars and subway vents every day – but smokers on the street make things even worse. "I mean, 50% of the litter on the street comes from cigarette butts because people never put them in the garbage," she says. "Smokers always put them out on the street and stamp on them with their feet." Margaret believes that being in an environment with a smoker is enough to affect her relationship with someone. She has a close friend whose mother has been a smoker for a long time. "My friend always complains that her room smells like cigarettes because of her mom's smoking. It just smells really really bad. It makes me not want to go over to her apartment either. I'm afraid – and she's afraid – that it's really bad for her if her mom is smoking all of the time around her."

Maintaining any kind of relationship with a smoker – whether it is a family member or a friend – seems nearly impossible to Margaret. She thinks it would be especially hard to stay friends with people who decided to smoke. "I'd try to help them quit, first of all, but I'd also be really scared that they would influence me to smoke, and then I'd probably not want to be as close to them anymore." She is thankful that she doesn't have any friends who smoke. From what she has noticed about smokers, she can easily see how it would interfere with a friend's ability to go out to dinner or to hang out and have fun. "If you smoked, you wouldn't be able to just sit down and relax. You'd always have to get up

DID YOU KNOW?

Many people might think that smoking is a social thing to do, but one study has suggested that **tobacco** may actually make you spend less time with your friends and more time alone. Teens and young adults who use tobacco may be more likely to develop **panic disorder, generalized anxiety disorder**, and **agoraphobia** (the fear of leaving home or going outdoors). Although further research is needed, the people who conducted this particular study think that smoking's negative effects on breathing and the damage **nicotine** does to the blood vessels that lead to the brain might explain why people who smoke are at risk for such anxiety disorders.[1]

and go out for a cigarette. It would always interrupt everything!" she exclaims.

Despite everything that Margaret hates about smoking – the health problems, the smell, the cloudy air, and the negative effects on appearance – she also knows that you can't just give up on someone if they smoke. She says that she would try to help a friend who smokes to quit by acting as a positive influence and by hanging around with them a lot. She says, "I'd want to try to help them and not leave them." She would want to make it clear to them that the sooner they quit, the longer they'll be happier in life.

Margaret knows that she has no reason to ever start smoking, even if someone or some movie told her it was the thing to do. "Smoking isn't cool at all because something cool is supposed to be something that is fun. How can something fun or cool ever come from something that's so bad for you?" This cool twelve-year-old would rather stick to dancing.

 In Margaret's own words ...

What do I think about smoking? Smoking is bad for you! Smoking is bad for you! Smoking is bad for you! End of story. There are thousands of reasons not to smoke. It smokes up your lungs. You could cop a stroke. It gets into your liver and your heart. Everyone knows you can't run or dance well if you smoke. Everything you do gets affected by your smoking. If those aren't good enough reasons, how about the fact that smokers smell? In fact, they smell bad. No one will like you. A smoker is unattractive, and has yellow teeth. They're not the type of person you would want to hang out with.

SMOKING STATS

About 80% of American 8th and 10th graders say that they prefer to date people who don't smoke.[2]

Alexis Bordeleau, 10

"There are a lot of reasons why I will never smoke," says Alexis. One of the main reasons is because cigarettes cause **cancer**. "Cancer is a very serious disease that can kill you," he explains. "Smoking makes your lungs dirty, and sometimes they turn all black. It also damages your heart, which can make you get sick in a lot of other ways," he adds.

Alexis loves the outdoors and playing sports – he especially enjoys football and hockey – which is another reason why he says he will never smoke. "Cigarettes make you worse at sports," he says. "When you smoke, you lose your breath much faster." Alexis brings up the subject of money too. "Cigarettes are expensive," he says. "So when you smoke, you have less money for things you enjoy, like vacations and trips, or even a car."

FAST FACTS

All tobacco products can cause **halitosis** (a serious case of having bad breath that smells like burnt tires), and yellow and brown teeth stains. One of the grossest effects of smoking cigarettes or using any other tobacco product is something called "smoker's tongue syndrome" – this happens when the tongue gets damaged and looks brown, black, and hairy! If you're brave enough, ask your dentist to show you pictures.[1]

But what really bothers Alexis about smoking, as he explains in his essay, is that it affects relationships between friends and family, and even between boyfriends and girlfriends. He doesn't understand why anyone would ever want to start such a stinky habit that makes you sick.

In Alexis's own words ...

Why I Don't Ever Want To Start Smoking

Cigarettes stink. People who smoke have really bad breath and they just smell bad. When you see someone, you can tell if they smoke because they'll have yellow teeth. I don't like talking with people who smoke because of how it changes their voices. People who smoke have weird voices. It's like their throats are always irritated.

I don't like to go to my friend Jean's house very much because his whole family smokes. It stinks in his house, and when I go there I also end up smelling like smoke, especially my hair. Jean's grandmother's name is Lorraine. She smokes too. If she were to tell me that she was going to quit, I would tell her that that would be a very good idea, and I would encourage her. I wouldn't tell her that it would be good because her house would stop smelling so bad, but I would tell her that she would have more energy, and that she could enjoy walks outside. I would also tell her that it's much better to breathe fresh air than it is to breathe in smoke.

When I was little, my father used to smoke too. I hope he'll never start again because I don't like people who smoke, and I would really worry about him (but I'd still love him anyway, that's for sure). If he started smoking again, I'd try and convince him to quit right away.

If someone asked me to smoke, even if it was my friend, I would say no. And if my friend wanted to force me to smoke, I would choose not to be their friend anymore. If I had a friend who told me that cigarettes are cool, I would warn them that once you start smoking, you will want to smoke all your life. I would also tell them that smoking is a lot like drugs. Right after you start smoking you might still feel full of energy, but after a while, you'll feel very tired. If my friends were sick and didn't have any energy, they wouldn't be able to play sports with me.

And no one should keep secrets from their parents. It's very bad to lie to your parents, because if you do, they won't be able to trust you anymore. And I wouldn't want friends who are liars either.

When I have a girlfriend, she definitely won't smoke. I would never be able to hug a girl who smokes. It's probably really gross to hug a girl who smells bad. And I wouldn't want to live in a house that always smells of smoke, because it would be bad for my health too. Even breathing secondhand smoke is bad for your health.

DID YOU KNOW?

Smoking can cause **impotence**, meaning that guys who smoke are less likely to be able to have children when they're older. The more they smoke, the more difficult it gets.[4]

WARNING
TOBACCO USE CAN MAKE YOU IMPOTENT
Cigarettes may cause sexual impotence due to decreased blood flow to the penis. This can prevent you from having an erection.
Health Canada

Licensed under Health Canada copyright.

A picture-based health warning that appears on cigarette packages in Canada.

Frédérique Bordeleau, 13

For Frédérique, also known as Frédo, friendship is very important. She is very loyal to her friends, who trust her and often confide in her.

Frédo is very creative and likes to write short stories. She started her first journal when she was only six. She's now part of a special arts program at her school, in which students are encouraged to express themselves through writing, music, theater, and graphic arts. Frédo felt that crafting a short story would be the best way to share her thoughts and feelings about smoking. Although her story is fictional, she believes that many kids her age start smoking in an effort to fit in and be cool.

 In Frédo's own words ...

I'm going to tell you the story of Camille, a 13-year-old girl who lives a normal life in Montreal. Camille has a lot of good friends, but that's not what interests her. What is constantly on her mind are the girls and boys in grade 10, but Camille is only in grade 8. Her dream is to be a part of their group. Every day, she watches them smoking this ignoble thing, this thing that kills and makes you unhappy, this thing that grabs at your spirit and doesn't let you go. This thing is called a cigarette. But Camille, naïve and innocent, thinks this group is cool because they smoke. One day, she decided to go and talk to them but didn't think that her friends would want her to. They begged her not to go and not to try smoking, but unfortunately Camille only had one thing on her mind: to prove that she was cool too.

Cool…a very complicated word. For some people, being cool means dressing well or being popular, but for poor Camille, being cool means smoking and hanging out with older kids. Without listening to her friends who were trying desperately to stop her, Camille approached the group of grade 10 students. Once she got close to them, she smelled that odor that makes you nauseous and suffocates you, that disgusting grayish smoke. But Camille didn't care.

"Yo!" said Camille, who wasn't very sure of herself. (She wanted to adapt herself to their language.)

"What do you want, minus?" said one girl as she coughed.

"Can I try?" responded Camille in a decided tone.

A boy held out a cigarette and laughed a little. Camille didn't even notice, and lit the cigarette with a lighter that another boy had given her while giving his friend a look. Without hesitation, she brought the cigarette to her mouth and inhaled. The moment the smoked passed through her throat and entered her lungs, Camille experienced a horrible feeling. She had the urge to vomit and she coughed suddenly while exhaling the horrible thick smoke. Everyone started to laugh, and Camille continued until she had finished the whole cigarette. She threw the last bit that was left on the ground, but the real Camille would never have done such a thing. The Camille that her friends knew was nice and kind. The Camille that her friends knew had hated cigarettes and drugs until the group of older kids arrived.

A boy with sunken red eyes, bad breath, and yellow teeth said to her, "Hey, you're cool!" as he opened a beer bottle.

The moment he uttered that sentence, Camille wanted to show him exactly what she was capable of and asked for another cigarette …

I could keep telling you Camille's story, but it would take too long. Most of the reasons not to smoke are here. In summary, this is why I do not want to smoke: because it's very bad and harmful for your health, it pollutes the air for those around you, it stinks, it takes a hold of you, and it's very hard to quit. For me, smoking is just a way to ruin your life, a way to ruin the air for your children, and a way to kill. Life is worth living, and a little roll of paper will not stop me from living my life healthfully and joyfully.

I accept myself as I am and I don't need to smoke to prove that I'm cool.

ACTIVIST MOMENTS

People may try to pressure you to smoke, but you and your friends can also work together to discourage smoking and make smoking uncool. In 1996, the Campaign for Tobacco Free Kids put on the first annual "Kick Butts Day," which proved that anyone can be an **activist.** The mission: for kids to prevent other kids from ever lighting up in the first place.[5]

Kick Butts Day (held on a different date each year) helps kids organize their own awesome events to raise awareness about the harmful effects of smoking. Kids across the country have held events like battles of the bands, track meets, carnivals, and marches for those who have lost loved ones to tobacco-related diseases. Kick Butts also provides information on how to propose a law against secondhand tobacco and how to create a Public Service Announcement (which means you get to speak out against tobacco *and* be on the radio!).[6]

There are many ways you can celebrate Kick Butts Day, so be creative! In 2006, a middle school in the United States made a display that consisted of 350 empty pairs of shoes – one for each life that is ended during a seven-hour school day by a smoking-related illness in the United States.[7]

INSTANT HISTORY FACTS

Efforts are being made all over the world to try to make it harder for young people to get cigarettes. For the last 100 years in the United Kingdom, tobacco could not legally be sold to anyone under 16. Now, the United Kingdom has decided to raise the **legal age** to 18, starting October 1, 2007.[8]

With this raise in age, the United Kingdom joins other countries, such as Canada, Australia, New Zealand, and the United States as places where **retailers** can only sell tobacco to people at least 18 years old.[9] In some American states, the legal age is 19 years old. In four Canadian provinces (Nova Scotia, New Brunswick, Ontario, and British Columbia), the legal age is also 19.[10]

But despite these laws, some cigarette **vendors** still sell cigarettes to minors anyway and are rarely fined. Young people are still given cigarettes and they still smoke. More than half of all young smokers usually buy cigarettes, either directly from retailers, vending machines, or other kids, or by giving money to others to buy the cigarettes for them.[11]

Young smokers can be punished just for **possession** of tobacco (owning tobacco and having control over what is done with it). For example, the Canadian province of Alberta has a law where anyone under 18 caught in possession of or caught using tobacco products can be charged with a $100 fine.[12] In the United States, 42 states have **youth possession laws**. In Pennsylvania, students caught with tobacco on school property are fined $50, plus up to $125 in court costs.[13] In Tucson, Arizona, a youth caught in possession of tobacco could have his or her driver's license suspended, and if they don't have a driver's license yet, they can be "locked out" from getting one until they turn 18.[14]

This is all important information to keep in mind if people ever pressure you to smoke. It could cost you in many ways!

Bianca Gurciullo, 12

When it gets warm in the summer, one of Bianca's favorite things to do is play outside with her two little sisters and her neighbor, Brandon. "I like to play pretend games," she says. "We usually pretend, like, we're a big family. The oldest of us pretend to be the parents to my little sisters." As a big sister in *real* life, Bianca knows that she sets an example for her sisters. She takes this responsibility super seriously, especially when it comes to influencing her siblings not to smoke. "If they were ever thinking about smoking, I would tell them all the bad things, like lung cancer, that can happen when you start," she says. "It's bad for you. The nicotine is really bad for your body," she explains. "Once you start, it's hard to stop."

Bianca knows just how addictive the nicotine in cigarettes is because of her aunt, who has been smoking for over twenty years. "She's tried to stop but she can't," Bianca says. "I worry about her because she looks older than she's supposed to." When she was younger, Bianca tried to help her aunt stop smoking. "I would tell her about all the bad things that happen ... I would try to get her to cut down. I would always take her cigarettes away from her and hide them."

Having a relative who smokes has made Bianca very aware of how *everyone* – not just the people who smoke – is affected by cigarettes, especially a smoker's family and friends. For one thing, everybody has to deal with the gross smell that comes from cigarettes. "My cousins' house always smells like smoke – it's really bad," Bianca complains. "My aunt always smells like smoke," she adds. "Even if she goes outside, she comes back with the smell on her. She takes, like, three showers a day!" More than anything, though, Bianca worries about her aunt's health. "I'm afraid she might die," she says. "I also worry about my cousins," she adds. "What if they lose their mom?"

When it comes to kids and smoking, Bianca believes that parents are a big influence on their children's decisions. "I think if the parents don't smoke, it sets an example for the kids. If the parents *do* smoke, then the kids might smoke." Bianca is happy that neither of her parents smokes and she looks to her mom and dad as role models. "They're the ones who always teach me what to do. They teach me to keep my body healthy."

FAST FACTS

Even some churches in Bangkok think smoking isn't cool. In 2007, they asked Catholics who smoke to quit during the 40 days of Lent, in the hopes that this will help people stop smoking for good. These churches believe that quitting the harmful habit will help parishioners be closer to God.[15]

Knowing all the harmful effects of cigarettes, Bianca is sure she will never even consider smoking. "It takes away from everyday life," she says. This ambitious girl has a lot of big plans for the future and she knows smoking won't help her achieve any of them. "I want to go to Italy and see the Colosseum," she says. "And when I'm older, I think I probably want to be a veterinarian or a writer." She has a lot of exciting dreams for the future, but for now, everyday life for Bianca means bike-riding, swimming, and playing with her sisters. There's no doubt that this smart anti-smoking big sister will set a great example for her siblings.

In Bianca's own words ...

I have something to say to everyone who reads this: smoking stinks and I have 10 reasons why people should never start. But first, I would like to tell you a little bit about why I'm so against it. When I was nine years old, I tried to get my aunts to stop smoking because I didn't want them to die. Every time I saw them smoke I would tell them to stop! I asked my aunt once why she smoked and she said it first started in high school (that was about 20 years ago), because she wanted to be cool, and her friends told her she wouldn't be cool if she didn't do it. Now, she's tried stopping but can't! This is why I will never start smoking – if your friends say you're not cool or are a chicken, change friends because no friend is worth it. Having no friend at all is better than having friends who smoke.

Here are my 10 reasons never to start smoking:

1) Smoking is bad for the environment. The air is polluted enough as it is with all the factories and cars.

2) It gives you lung cancer (there are enough ways to get cancer in this world without adding smoking to the list!) and it makes your heart and lungs all black (and it shrinks your lungs also).

3) It gives you bad breath and turns your teeth yellow – gross! (The first thing my dad said when he first met my mom

– who was smoking at the time – was, "Yuck, your mouth must taste like a chimney!" My mom quit smoking right then and there.)

4) There are all kinds of poison and garbage in cigarettes, including nicotine, which is highly addictive. So it's very hard to stop once you start. Of course, the cigarette companies do that so they can make more money killing people.

5) Smoking is very expensive. That money could be spent on more fun things like movies, outings, clothes.

6) Smoking makes you sick and lands you in the hospital, so more money is wasted on medication, treatments, patches ... but now you're even suffering on top of that!

7) Smoking leads to other kinds of drugs. In the same way you get addicted to cigarettes, you get addicted to other drugs, and doing drugs leads straight to your death.

8) Smoking makes your skin gray, thins out your hair, gets you sick faster, ages you faster than you should age, and is very unhealthy!

9) Smoking is very hard to stop, so it hooks you for life. My aunt started because of her friends – to be cool – now she can't stop. It's stronger than her.

10) To sum it all up: smoking is gross, bad for you, addictive, bad for the air we breathe, destroys your immune system,

and costs so much money for something that will eventually kill you. I cannot understand why anyone would even start. We have the choice to be stronger, healthier, and live longer.

We should close down the cigarette companies so we will never have to go through what past generations have gone through. That's the only solution I can think of to eliminate all these problems. Remember: Never start smoking! Smoking stinks! Smoking will kill you! No friend is worth your health.

DID YOU KNOW?

Smoking may be a "**gateway**" to illegal drug use, and the earlier someone experiments with **tobacco**, the more likely he or she is to use marijuana, cocaine, heroin, and other life-threatening, illegal drugs.[16]

FAMILY'S HEALTH
+
SECONDHAND SMOKE

Cassidy Anne Sauvé, 9

Although she was only six when her grandfather was diagnosed with **lung cancer**, Cassidy still remembers how smoking made him sick, and she has taken that lesson seriously. Even though her grandmother stopped smoking when her grandfather died, Cassidy still worries about the effects of **secondhand smoke** and believes that being exposed to smoke can make it harder for other people to quit. Cassidy would never make cigarettes a part of her life because she knows how important it is to stay healthy. After all, she needs the energy to play catch with her younger brother Hayden (who is six years old), and to try out for the indoor soccer team this fall – she hopes to be goalie. Cassidy is sharing her story with the hope that by speaking out against smoking, other people won't have to lose someone they love like she did.

 In Cassidy's own words ...

Smoking & How it Affects Others

My grandparents (my dad's mom and dad) used to smoke for as long as I could remember. We live in Alberta and they live in British Columbia. When they visited us, they would go outside to smoke, but I had to stay in the house and look out the window. I always wished I could be outside with them because I didn't get to see them very often. They would not let me come outside because they wanted to protect me from their smoke. I didn't understand why I couldn't come out, and it made me feel sad.

I was not even three when I pretended to smoke with candy sticks. I did this because I wanted to be like my grandparents. Adults shouldn't smoke around kids because it gives kids the wrong idea. It makes them think it is okay because older people are doing it. My grandparents knew it was bad for them but they kept on doing it. Now I wished they had never started smoking. I will never smoke.

My grandpa got lung cancer when I was six and my brother, Hayden, was four. We went to visit Grandpa in the hospital one time and there were lots of other sick people there because they smoked. It was smelly and freaky to be there with all those sick people. When I first went in to see my grandpa, I wanted to cast a spell on him so he wouldn't be sick anymore. I didn't ever want to have to go there again, even though it was my grandpa. The other people in his room were coughing so hard it sounded like they were throwing up. It was freaky and I was very scared. I wanted to be with Grandpa but it freaked me out too much. My grandpa died five months later on Thanksgiving.

I asked my mom why people smoke if it's bad for them. She said they just don't know better. But I know better. I know that smoking kills people. It killed Grandpa. It could kill other people in my family.

The government makes people who make cigarettes write what smoking does to you on the cigarette pack. One warning says 45,000 Canadians die every year from tobacco and smoking. If the people who make cigarettes know what it does to people, they should stop making cigarettes. They kill people and make money. It's like murder.

The government lets people sell cigarettes. This means they don't care about our health either. Not all people in the government feel this way. But they need to stand up for everyone! People who smoke can kill other people by smoking around them.

Even though my grandpa is gone, my memories of what smoking did to him teach me the lesson not to ever smoke. I hope everyone reading my story gets the message to never smoke.

FAST FACTS

Cigarette smoking within families can result in a vicious smoke ring. For example, whether your parents smoke or not makes a big difference in whether you smoke. Children of smokers are almost twice as likely to smoke than children with parents who don't smoke.[1] And if you start smoking, you influence your siblings. There is a greater chance that your brothers and sisters will smoke if you do.[2]

Licensed under Health Canada copyright.

WARNING
CHILDREN SEE CHILDREN DO

Your children are twice as likely to smoke if you do. Half of all premature deaths among life-long smokers result from tobacco use.

Health Canada

A picture-based health warning that appears on cigarette packages in Canada.

INSTANT HISTORY FACTS

Can you believe that smoking was once allowed almost everywhere – even on airplanes? Commercial airplanes didn't start to **ban** smoking on flights until 1988.[3]

Patty Young, who was a flight attendant for 36 years, is one activist who fought hard to make this change. She testified in 1980 before **Congress** to persuade lawmakers to end smoking on flights, and organized a major **lawsuit** for flight attendants who had the lungs of smokers even though they didn't smoke. Patty and her nonsmoking co-workers were getting sick from all the smoke in the small space of an airplane – one of her co-workers had even died of **lung cancer** at age 28. Both of Patty's parents were smokers who died of lung cancer, and she knew that something had to be done.[4]

It has now been 20 years since the smoking ban on airplanes, and many new smoking bans have been put into effect. There are bans on smoking in restaurants, beaches, sports grounds, and parks in countries all over the world, in order to help stop the spread of **secondhand smoke**, which contains many of the same chemicals that smokers inhale. Over 250 chemicals in secondhand smoke are toxic or cause cancer. Secondhand smoke includes both the smoke that is released from the burning end of a cigarette and the smoke that is **exhaled** by the smoker.[5]

Adam G. Morgan, 12

Adam has many reasons not to smoke. He values time with his family and would never have the heart to smoke around his two-year-old sister. Being a great older brother and role model is one of the most important things to him. Adam thinks that kids his age start smoking because "everyone's minds are all 'gibbled' up, and they have too much on their plates." As a result, he says, they turn to cigarettes as a way to relieve stress, or to make themselves look older and more mature. Adam's own plate is full with acting in school plays and musicals, and being part of his school's Junior Advisory Book Committee. However, no matter how busy he may be, Adam says he'd never turn to cigarettes. He is all too familiar with the damage and pain that result from smoking. Adam was inspired to write this essay for his father, a smoker, who he hopes will one day find the strength to quit. Adam wants to tell everyone who will listen that cigarettes aren't worth the pain that they cause.

SMOKING STATS

- If two parents each smoked half a pack of cigarettes a day at home, in one year a child may be exposed to the smoke from over 7,000 cigarettes.[6]

- Secondhand smoke has been labeled as a "Class A" cancer-causing substance in the United States. Class A is considered the most dangerous type of cancer agent and there is no known safe level of exposure.[7]

In Adam's own words ...

My Reasons for Choosing Not To Smoke

Cigarettes stink! For starters, the smell of the stuff is absolutely deplorable and there are enough chemicals in cigarettes to kill an African elephant. Worst of all, tobacco can cause many health problems including **cancer** and **emphysema**, two fatal diseases. Can you imagine having to live with dangerous cells that slowly eat away at your lungs? Can you imagine having to sit in a hospital bed for the short remainder of your agony-plagued life and have some machine breathe for you? I certainly can't, and I don't intend to live up to that fantasy!

Though some people may already know these terrible facts, I can't help restating them. Choosing not to smoke is one of the best decisions an individual can make in his or her life. Not smoking can open up many areas in your life. Several jobs today require that their employees do not smoke, so being smoke-free can open up new career opportunities. More and more people today are turning away from smoking, so if I start to smoke, I could lose some of my friends (I am proud to say that none of my friends or acquaintances smoke cigarettes). Also, most of Canada has banned smoking in public places. Cigarettes contain nicotine, a malevolently seductive and extremely addictive chemical to "keep hold" of tobacco buyers. Can YOU add two and two together here? You're at dinner with your family and you have to go for a smoke. You *really* need to go for a smoke, but the sign on the front door of the restaurant says "No Smoking on Restaurant Property." Why would you want to start something that is illegal to enjoy in the company of others?

I have never been interested in lighting a cigarette. No lie. I just can't imagine the thought of pulling out a cig and sticking it in my mouth. To me, it would be like sucking on a gas nozzle! Worst of all is the fact that hundreds of poisonous chemicals are burning while a cigarette is in your mouth. Personally, I have no understanding as to how people are attracted to these things. People look like babies going around with pacifiers.

Cigarettes are some of the most expensive things in the world. At almost ten dollars a pack (in Canada), they are a huge waste of money. I usually make about ten dollars a week in allowance. If I got addicted to cigarettes now, at twelve years old, I probably wouldn't be able to afford any other things that I might want for myself. Under no circumstances would I just chuck all that moolah down the drain and into the river! Yet if you try smoking, the tobacco company grabs you by the collar by adding our old pal **nicotine** into the mix. You see, the more addicted you are, the more tobacco companies will profit from your forced patronage. When you are talking about smoking, remember this: The tobacco industry is only interested in $$$, $$$, and more $$$!

I don't think I could ever be attracted to someone who smokes. If I had a friend or girlfriend who smoked cigarettes, I would still like them, but I would never like the smoke. Smoking doesn't make you a better or worse person; it just

WARNING

YOU'RE NOT THE ONLY ONE SMOKING THIS CIGARETTE

The smoke from a cigarette is not just inhaled by the smoker. It becomes second-hand smoke, which contains more than 50 cancer-causing agents.

Health Canada

A picture-based health warning that appears on cigarette packages in Canada.

means that you have made a bad decision. If a friend or loved one around you smokes, ask them why they started. They'll probably tell you why. Perhaps you can avoid smoking by staying away from the things that made that person start to smoke, and break the cycle.

The most compelling reason for why I have chosen not to smoke is personal. Unfortunately, my father smokes and it has taken a gruesome toll on him. Two years ago he suffered a massive stroke due to the harmful effects of smoking. Today, he still uses a walker to get around and he cannot work. My father told me that smoking is the worst thing he ever started and even though he lives with the effects of this mistake every day, he remains in the grip of this 35-year-long addiction. This addiction has hurt our family and I don't want it to hurt yours. I beg you, just please don't start. Smoking will put your life in a downward spiral and land you in a deep hole you won't be able to get out of.

Justin Kvadas, 10

Justin Kvadas is famous; people recognize him on the streets as the mastermind behind the proposal for his state of Connecticut to ban smoking in cars when children are present. He has to admit that "it's cool" to be a celebrity.

It all started when Justin's mom was driving him home from his tae kwon do class, where – get this – he is only one level away from his black belt. He was looking at the drivers on the road and he thought, *people aren't supposed to eat or drink or talk on the phone when they're driving, so why can people smoke?* Justin thought about how dangerous smoking is, and wanted to tell adults that their smoking is harming kids and that it needs to stop. He went to his State Representative and was told he should start a **petition**, which he did. He gathered over 200 signatures.

SMOKING STATS

Every year 5 million smokers in the world die.[8] But smokers are not only harming themselves – at least 53,000 innocent nonsmokers are killed from secondhand tobacco smoke every year in the United States alone.[9]

Justin appeared on TVs all across America when he testified in court to support the **bill** that he initiated. His mom, dad, little sister, grandparents, aunt, close family friends, and the three 5th grade classes from his school, as well as the teachers and the principal, all came to stand behind him. Two of his classmates also spoke in front of the legislation in support of his bill.

Justin's mom warned him that not everyone would want to stop smoking in their cars or would want a kid telling them what to do, but Justin's a fearless crusader against secondhand smoke – an activist who will keep working for change until it happens.

 In Justin's own words ...

On February 6, 2007, I testified in front of the Select Committee on Children at the Legislation Office in Connecticut in support of bill # 5204. This bill, if passed, will make it illegal to smoke in a vehicle if there is a child under the age of seven, or under 60 pounds, present.

It is dangerous for all children to be exposed to secondhand smoke but it's even more dangerous to small children. These children need protection from smokers. They can have permanent damage to their bodies from secondhand smoke that will harm them for life and shorten their life span. I want to help those children who cannot speak for themselves.

Adults in our schools and homes have told us that smoke causes cancer, lung disease, and is very dangerous to our health. There are adults who smoke and want the freedom to do this wherever they want. Who is going to stop these adults from harming small children with their smoking? We need to have a law to prevent this and protect children. It's our turn to educate the adults with this law.

So I'd like to share some facts with you about the dangers of secondhand smoke on children. I got these facts from the American Heart Association and the Environmental Protection Agency.

- When you are in a car there is only so much air to breathe. Children who spend one hour in an extremely smoky room inhale enough toxic chemicals to equal smoking 10 cigarettes.

- The dangers of secondhand smoke are worse for children. Not only are their bodies still developing, but also their breathing rates are faster than adults' breathing rates are. Adults breathe 14 to 18 times per minute while children breathe between 20 and 60 times per minute. This results in a higher concentration of toxins in the lungs of a young person who is surrounded by smoke.

- Children who breathe in secondhand smoke are more likely to suffer from dental cavities and ear infections.

- An estimated 35,000 to 62,000 deaths each year are caused by heart disease in people who are not current smokers but who are exposed to secondhand smoke.

I urged the committee to pass a law to ban smoking in cars. This is a change that would improve the quality of life for everyone. But most importantly, for those who cannot stick up for themselves. Isn't that what making a law is all about? I am pleased to announce that the bill has passed the Select Committee on Children by a vote of 6 to 3. The bill will now go to the Committee on Judiciary. If passed there, it will have to go up against two more Committees before becoming a new law. We hope it will make it through all the Committees before the end of the Legislation session in June. If not, I will continue to try until it passes.

ACTIVIST MOMENTS

In 2004, Justin Kvadas from the United States, only nine years old at the time, initiated a **bill** to change the law in his state of Connecticut to better protect young children from **secondhand smoke**. Justin thought that there should be a **ban** on smoking in the private realm, such as in cars, because secondhand smoke is especially harmful to children. Children are likely to suffer from **pneumonia**, **bronchitis**, and other **lung diseases** if exposed to high levels of secondhand smoke.[10] Justin testified in February 2007 in support of his bill and is waiting for it to be passed. Read more about Justin on pages 54-56.

Other people have initiated similar laws in other states. Bans on smoking in cars are already in place in Arkansas, Louisiana, and Bangor (Maine).[11] You can help to create nonsmoking environments too by being a polite activist in your own car and your own home. If someone in your family smokes, you can let them know that you are worried about their health and yours because smoke affects you too. You can suggest healthy alternatives that you can do together, like shooting hoops, taking a walk, or playing checkers. See page 189 for places to contact for more information about how to help friends and loved ones quit.

Merlin Lefebvre, 9

Nine-year-old Merlin Lefebvre likes to have fun. He loves video games and enjoys playing with his dog, Java, a boisterous three-year-old Boxer. Merlin likes to read, too, and just finished *The Uncle Duncle Chronicles*, his new favorite book. And like any kid his age, Merlin loves computers. He doesn't watch a lot of TV, but he makes sure never to miss his two favorite shows – *Mythbusters* and *The Amazing Race*. Add some Chinese noodles to the list and you've just described a perfect day for Merlin. The one activity that will never be a part of this list, however, is smoking. Merlin's mother and step-father both smoke, and he hates it.

DID YOU KNOW?

Secondhand smoke clings to rugs, curtains, clothes, food, and furniture, and it can last there for days, weeks, and even months later. Some parents think that it's all right to smoke in the house when their children aren't around or when they're in the next room, but secondhand smoke spreads easily from one room to another even if the door is closed.[12]

"My mom and my step-dad both smoke," he explains. "It really bothers me because it stinks and I don't want to smell like smoke." Merlin's mom and step-dad only smoke on the back porch, and never inside the apartment, and never around Merlin. "But I can *still* smell it," he says. "And it smells bad."

When asked what bothers him the most about cigarettes, he responds, *"C'est des niaiseries"* – a Québécois

DON'T POISON US

WARNING: Second-hand smoke contains carbon monoxide, ammonia, formaldehyde, benzo[a]pyrene and nitrosamines. These chemicals can harm your children.

Health Canada

A picture-based health warning that appears on cigarette packages in Canada.

expression that means "it's foolish." "So many people smoke, and then they get sick from cancer," he says. Merlin worries about the influence smokers have as well: "Kids see other people smoking, so they start, and then they might get sick too."

Merlin is concerned about his mother's health. "I worry a lot that she will get sick," he says. She has quit smoking before, but she recently started again. Merlin is very close with his mother, and tells her often that all he wants is for her to stop. She has promised to quit once and for all. They'll be moving into a new house soon, and Merlin really hopes that this will be even more of a reason for his mom and step-dad to quit – he doesn't want their new house to smell like smoke too.

Merlin thinks the best way to quit smoking is not to start in the first place. "It smells bad, makes you sick, and doesn't look like it tastes very good," he explains. If someone were to ask him to try a cigarette, Merlin, who is determined to never ever start smoking, would simply answer, "*No.* I don't want cancer!" He just doesn't understand why people would smoke. "*C'est des niaiseries*," he says again. "Smoking can stop you from doing the things you like to do. You can't do anything fun if you're stuck in a hospital."

Merlin has simple, straightforward advice for those who smoke: "*Stop Smoking!*" And for those who are trying to quit, like his mom, Merlin is encouraging. "Go for it!" he says. "Don't give up!" To anyone who's thinking about making cigarettes a habit, he says, "Please don't smoke – it's just not worth it."

DID YOU KNOW?

Pets are affected by smoking too! **Secondhand smoke** can cause **cancer** in cats and dogs. Cats and dogs don't just breathe smoke through their mouths – they also swallow it when they clean themselves with their tongues and lick the smoke particles that get trapped in their fur.[13]

ADDICTION

Makayla Power, 11

Makayla knows all the reasons not to smoke from listening to the news, reading the paper, and talking to her mom. However, her friendship with her cousin is more influential than any statistic. Watching her cousin struggle with a nicotine addiction made Makayla realize that she never wants to try smoking – not even once. "My cousin started smoking when she was twelve years old because all of her friends were doing it," Makayla says. "People were selling cigarettes at school, and her brother, sister, and dad all smoked, so it was even harder for her not to pick up the habit." Makayla's aunt convinced her cousin to try to quit. Though it wasn't easy, she managed to be smoke-free for a while. But, as Makayla explains, her cousin is having trouble breaking her addiction to cigarettes for good.

 In Makayla's own words ...

My cousin is almost 20 now and she smokes again. She says if she never started smoking in grade six, she wouldn't be smoking now. She really regrets it. Smoking is hard to quit and she tried a couple times. Whenever she takes a cigarette out and lights it she tells me, "If I ever catch you smoking I'm going to kick your butt because smoking is very bad, and I don't know why I picked it up."

Smoking kills 1,200 people a day (kidshealth.com). Smoking is very expensive. $10 a day (if you smoke a pack a day), $70 a week, $300 a month, and $3,650 a year. That's how much money you spend on cigarettes. People might not think they spend that much money on cigarettes but it's true. There are over 4,000 chemicals in a cigarette: tar, nicotine, acetone, ammonia, benzene, cadmium, carbon monoxide, and way more. Because of these chemicals, cigarettes are so addictive.

The health care costs are rising because of all the sickness that smoking is causing. Smoking causes lung cancer, heart disease, tooth and gum disease, asthma, and other diseases.

Now smoking in public places is banned because of secondhand smoke. The town where I live is behind in this movement, but is in the process of making changes. These changes are a good idea because people can still get affected from the secondhand smoke, and it's nice to go to restaurants with no smoking.

Smoking is a bad thing and it's one of the stupidest things you can ever do, so why do it?

DID YOU KNOW?

Nicotine is a liquid drug found in tobacco leaves. When a cigarette is lit, the nicotine evaporates and attaches to the tobacco smoke that is inhaled by the smoker.[1] Whether someone smokes, chews, or sniffs tobacco, nicotine from the tobacco travels to the brain and causes addiction. Cigarettes contain about 10 milligrams of nicotine, and 1 to 4 milligrams of nicotine from each cigarette is absorbed into the lungs.[2] Nicotine is the drug in tobacco that makes the body crave more cigarettes and keeps people smoking.

INSTANT HISTORY FACTS

- The **tobacco** plant was first grown and used in the Americas in 6000 BC. In 1493, Christopher Columbus discovered tobacco when he traveled to Cuba. He brought it back with him to Europe. One hundred and fifty years later, tobacco was being used around the world. In the 1700s, **snuff** was commonly used, and in the 1800s, **cigars** were more popular. That changed in 1881 when a machine to make cigarettes was invented. Manufactured cigarettes then caught on.[3]

- In 1988, the US Surgeon General concluded that tobacco is addictive, and that nicotine is the drug in tobacco that causes addiction.[4] In 1995, it was discovered that cigarette companies add ammonia to boost the effects of nicotine, allowing for more nicotine to get absorbed into the smoker's body. This makes the cigarette more addictive.[5]

- Cigarettes are continuing to change. A 2007 report found that the nicotine absorbed into the lungs from cigarettes has increased over 10% on average from 1998 to 2005.[6] The investigators found an increase in nicotine in all of the major types of cigarettes, including brands that are regular, light, medium, ultralight, mentholated, and non-mentholated.[7] Though more research needs to be done, it is thought that these increases in nicotine could make cigarettes even more addictive than they ever were before.[8]

Jamie Lawrence, 12

Jamie is strong, but she knows that she isn't strong enough to fight a smoking addiction. Some kids often think that they are able to resist a cigarette addiction, or that they could stop smoking at any time, but Jamie knows that nicotine has a powerful hold on the body and mind. She says people should remember that they can't take back their first cigarette. Jamie wants others to know that they're never too young to become addicted to tobacco, and that people shouldn't believe anyone who tries to tell them that smoking is no big deal. Also, Jamie points out that being addicted to cigarettes means that you wouldn't have the strength to play sports or run. Jamie could never let

SMOKING STATS

About 70% of smokers say that they want to quit, but each year only 4.7% of smokers can do it. Almost all smokers start their cigarette habit when they are under 18 years old.[9]

something like smoking hold her back – she enjoys staying active by playing badminton and figure skating. As the youngest of six kids, Jamie is lucky that she never had to deal with a smoking addiction at home, and is happy that her mother quit smoking before Jamie was born.

In Jamie's own words ...

Is it time??

It's really hard to quit smoking!! Some say it is the hardest thing to do in life. Mainly because half of the time people are trying to quit, they are quitting because they are pressured by a family member or even a friend, but they themselves don't want to. There is a saying that suffering often brings great rewards, and you know this time that if you quit, that's what's going to happen. You have to want to quit smoking to actually quit. Some people think they don't want to smoke but they don't know for sure, so they waste all of their time trying to make the choice whether they want to or not. When you want to quit smoking, you have to quit very quickly because a cigarette can do a lot of damage in one day to your lungs. You may not have enough time to decide whether you want to quit or not. Did you know that smoking causes emphysema, strokes, heart attacks, cancers of the lungs, throat, esophagus, mouth, larynx, cervix, pancreas, and kidneys?

If you tell yourself the reasons that you want to quit, it's much easier to quit. It is not hard to think of a reason or two because there are so many chemicals. Most people think they know how bad smoking can be, but there are over 4,000 chemicals in one individual cigarette. Of the 4,000 chemicals there are 43 carcinogens that are known to cause cancer in humans. There are a lot of things out in the world that are illegal to sell, but cigarettes are one of the few products that they can sell you and it's still legal.

Why do people smoke? They are pressured into it by peers to be part of a crowd. They say it is relaxing. After 20 years of smoking people still think it is relaxing to smoke. People also start smoking because they are feeling stressed, angry, or are just upset. You can get over being stressed and upset but you cannot take back smoking. There is a very high chance that you'll get addicted.

People who smoke will most likely get addicted to nicotine. It is a drug that they put in the cigarette that has a bunch of different effects and can affect the body at the same time! After one puff of the cigarette the nicotine begins to work on your central nervous system, brain, and other parts of the body. Most people say that nicotine is the main ingredient in cigarettes that makes smoking so relaxing. Although it may seem that it does relax you, it doesn't. The nicotine actually stimulates your system. Now you are probably thinking why does nicotine make you feel so good and relaxed? It is because nicotine affects chemicals in your brain and after one puff you can sometimes feel good for a while and that is also usually why smokers view smoking as a stress reliever.

Smoking is the #1 preventable cause of death in the United States.

ACTIVIST MOMENTS

In 1997, Debi Austin, a laryngectomy patient, filmed a commercial to show people just how addictive cigarettes are. Debi had to have a laryngectomy because she got laryngeal cancer from smoking. Laryngectomy patients have their **larynx** surgically removed and a hole put in their neck, called a stoma, and they have to breathe through the hole. In the commercial, Debi smokes through the stoma because she can no longer smoke through her mouth. Debi explains that the tobacco industry lied to her by saying that tobacco wasn't addictive, and says that she can't stop smoking even after getting cancer and a laryngectomy, because she's addicted.[10]

Debi isn't the only one who has had smoking-related surgery and still smokes afterward. About 40% of people who have laryngectomies start smoking soon after the operation, and about 50% of lung cancer patients smoke after having surgery.[11] Debi allowed herself to be filmed in order to let viewers see how serious addiction is. It was effective – people remembered her commercial more than any other smoking commercial up until that time.[12]

Terri-Lynn Critch, 13

Terri-Lynn knows firsthand how difficult it is to give up something as addictive as nicotine. Both her mom and grandfather started smoking at age 15 and can't quit, despite the family's history of lung cancer, heart disease, stroke, and asthma. Terri-Lynn and her sister have had asthma since birth, possibly as a result of being exposed to secondhand smoke before they were born. Asthma is a disease in which the airways get irritated and swell up. It can make it difficult to breath and cause coughing or wheezing. Terri-Lynn says, "Asthma doesn't stop me from playing sports, but it means I have to take breaks sometimes." She can't always run as far or as fast as she would like, but she stays active. In the winter, she enjoys snowboarding on the hills near her house, and in the summer she plays soccer. Terri-Lynn and her sister have decided that they will never start smoking so that they will never get addicted and compromise their health.

 In Terri-Lynn's own words ...

When my grandpa turned 15 years old he started smoking. He then got addicted to it and kept on smoking. When he turned about 28 he had a heart attack. His wife called 911 and rushed him to the hospital. A couple of days later the doctor came in and told him he needed to use a puffer [an inhaler] every day.

A couple of years later he had another heart attack and went to the hospital where they told him he had heart disease. That same day his dad died from lung cancer and heart disease. He was scared he was going to die from heart disease. He tried to quit but it didn't work.

A couple of months later my grandma found out she was pregnant. She was so happy that she went and bought a whole bunch of baby stuff. She went to the hospital a couple of days later just to see if the baby was okay. The doctor came in to give her an ultrasound and returned an hour later and told her she had a miscarriage. She cried for a whole week.

Then about a year later she found out she was pregnant again. She was afraid she was going to have another miscarriage. Every two weeks she went to the hospital just to see if the baby was okay. Nine months later she had a baby girl named Cindy (my mom). The doctor said that because my grandma smoked, the baby had asthma. My grandma couldn't stop smoking because she was addicted to it.

When Cindy turned 15 her mom and dad were smoking around her all the time. Cindy thought it was pretty cool so when her mom was sleeping she took a smoke from her mom's purse and started smoking. She decided she liked it, so she went back inside and got about five or six more and hid them under her bed.

In the morning, she took the smokes out from under her bed and put them in her purse. Cindy told her mom she was going to go hang out with her friends, but instead she went to the park and started smoking.

Every day until she was old enough to buy her own smokes, she took them from her mom's purse and smoked them. When she turned 24, the doctor told her that she was pregnant. She was scared that her baby was going to die or have lung cancer or something like that. Nine months later she had a little girl named Stacey. The doctors told her the baby had asthma. Cindy never smoked around Stacey because she never wanted her to start.

Two years later, Cindy went to the doctor because she wasn't feeling well. The doctors told her she was pregnant again. Nine months later she had a little girl named Terri-Lynn (Me!). I also had asthma.

I am now 13 and my sister is 15, and I have never tried smoking – same with my sister. My mom still smokes, she is 34. NEVER try smoking. It can cause lung cancer, heart attacks, strokes, sudden infant death syndrome, and much, much more.

FAST FACTS

People who start smoking usually feel sick right away. New smokers often start coughing and gagging, get headaches, and feel dizzy and **nauseated**.[13] *It may only take weeks or even days for young smokers to get addicted.*[14]

DID YOU KNOW?

Nicotine reaches the brain in fewer than ten seconds after cigarette smoke is inhaled.[15] After someone inhales cigarette smoke, the nicotine is pulled into the lungs, where it is absorbed into the blood. When it gets to the brain, it stimulates the nervous system, and this causes increases in **heart rate** and **blood pressure**, squeezing and tightening small blood vessels under the skin.[16]

Jill Schutjer's 7th Grade Class

Mrs. Schutjer's 7th grade language arts class has a lot to say about tobacco addiction and why everyone should avoid cigarettes altogether. Her students researched the tobacco industry and cigarettes, and many were shocked by what they learned. Most of the class even brought home statistics to share with their parents who smoke. The students then wrote about their thoughts on cigarettes and the importance of making smart choices when it comes to health. They hope that their words will influence others not to start smoking. Working on this project, they say, will make them all think twice before ever lighting up. (Look for more of their opinions on pages 94 & 111.)

 In their own words ...

Gabe Thomsen, 13

Smoking is very addictive. It can get so addictive that you can go through a carton a day. That is a lot of money when you add up how much it can cost over a period of time. If you go to a movie or a sports game, when you go outside to smoke you might have to buy another ticket to get back in to finish watching the game or the movie that you and somebody else might have gone to. Some people say that they can quit any time that they want, but it turns out to be way too hard for them to do. Smoking can become that addictive.

Kelsey Ufford, 13

One reason not to smoke is that when you start, you can't stop. You may think you can, but you can't. Your brain craves nicotine when you start. If your brain craves nicotine and you don't give in to it then your brain goes mad! You will be crabby and you'll make everyone around you crabby. So, you may think you can stop but really, you can't. If getting lung cancer, smelly breath, yellow teeth, having to worry about your kids smelling like smoke everywhere you go, having to talk through a machine, having your lungs collapse, getting pneumonia, or even dying sounds fun, then I'm really worried for you. You can have uncontrollable coughing spells, and all that coughing will hurt your throat. Your lungs will go bad and you'll be breathless.

Zac Ree, 13

Smoking is addictive. You start and you can't stop. You can try to stop, but very few people are able to stop. A person I know tried to stop, but after one week he had to have one smoke. When you try to stop smoking you might try to use the special gum or chew sunflower seeds. If you start to smoke, you will regret it, so don't even think about starting to smoke.

FAST FACTS

Tobacco companies have said that cigarettes are only as addictive as television, coffee, and M&Ms. One **Big Tobacco** executive even said in court that he believed that cigarettes were only as addictive as Gummy Bears. He said, "I love Gummy Bears. I don't like it when I don't eat my Gummy Bears, but I'm certainly not addicted to them."[17]

In fact, nicotine is one of the most addictive substances known to man. About 8 out of every 10 people who try smoking just once get hooked.[18] A highly addicted smoker will smoke 25 cigarettes a day, and needs to smoke within 30 minutes after waking up in the morning.[19] What makes these facts even more alarming is that tobacco has been found to be more harmful than illegal drugs like marijuana or ecstasy[20], and more addictive than heroin or cocaine.[21]

DID YOU KNOW?

Nicotine is not only addictive, but it is also extremely poisonous. Nicotine is used as a **pesticide** on crops, which kills insects and birds.[22] It is even used in darts to knock down elephants and paralyze them.[23] Just one drop of pure nicotine would kill a person.[24] Every year, young children go to the hospital after eating cigarettes or cigarette butts. The nicotine in just one cigarette is enough to make a toddler very sick.[25]

Kayla Belec, 13

Kayla's personal experience with smoking addiction in her family has changed her life, and has helped her make the right decisions when it comes to tobacco. Having seen the hold that smoking has on her grandmother, Kayla thinks twice when someone offers her a cigarette. Kayla believes that smoking can lead you to make bad choices and wants people to know that there are better ways to spend your time than puffing it away. Her time, she says, is best spent hanging out with friends, listening to emo, punk and techno music, and expressing herself through poetry and her acoustic guitar. She was inspired to put her family's regrets about smoking into writing and decided to include a poem here. Kayla thinks that no one should have to worry about the effects of smoking. She wants everyone to know that not smoking today means that you won't have to worry about serious health problems tomorrow.

FAST FACTS

In addition to all of the serious health problems smoking causes, a cigarette addiction might make a student's grades slip. It may take longer for students who start smoking at an early age to understand information and it may be harder for them to remember it.[26]

 In Kayla's own words ...

We are all aware that smoking is bad for you. Believe it or not, even smokers know. We warn them about what could happen in the future and we tell them that they should quit. Well, they know. Pretty much everyone does try to quit. It's really hard. Some say it's as bad as not eating. I can believe that. There are more than 4,000 chemicals in one single cigarette. That 4,000 is just another way to say goodbye to your life. I mean, sure, some people stay alive, but not all. A lot of people end up getting cancer of some sort. Why? Because they didn't quit smoking soon enough.

At least one person in everyone's family smokes. For instance, my grandmother smokes. It kills me just to think of what could happen to her. She's been smoking for most of her life, and every day I think "Oh my, will she die? Will she get sick?" It could happen in the blink of an eye, or in a decade. I worry for her all the time. She's trying to quit and she tells me how hard it is for her. I believe in her. I believe that *every* single person who smokes can quit in order to save their lives. My great grandparents died when I was about 8 years old due to smoking. My great grandfather got lung cancer. A couple of months later, my great grandmother had bad lungs. I think that when they found out they were sick, they regretted that they didn't try hard enough to quit.

Think twice about it when someone asks you to try a cigarette or any kind of drug. Think about the future and how you can stop the bad from happening now.

When you walk into that school yard
You smell peer pressure.
When you walk up to the cool kids
You smell smoke.
When they walk up to you,
Asking "Want a smoke?"
You simply reply with a,
"Uh, okay?"

You inhale
You exhale
You breathe
You cough
You smoke more
Until the day you die.

Damn regrets
Is all you think of
When you look at the doctor
In the eye
When he breaks the bad news to you.
That night
When you lie in a puddle of your life-time tears
You can't think of anything but
"What if I said no to that smoke?"

– Kayla Belec

INSTANT HISTORY FACTS

"Light" and "ultralight" cigarettes were introduced in the 1950s and 1960s because smokers were beginning to understand that smoking threatened their health. Tobacco companies told the public that these new types of cigarettes were healthier,[27] but this was not the truth. Fast-forward to 2001 when studies show that these types of cigarettes do not reduce the health risks of smoking and can be as **addictive** and deadly as regular cigarettes.[28]

DID YOU KNOW?

Nicotine stimulates **neurons** so that they release **dopamine**, which creates feelings of pleasure.[29] Smokers become addicted to nicotine because they want those pleasurable feelings, but research suggests that nicotine can actually make it harder for the brain to feel pleasure. If nicotine is used over time, more and more nicotine is needed for the smoker just to feel normal. In only 40 minutes, many of the effects of nicotine are gone, and smokers want more.[30] They start to feel depressed and experience withdrawal – they get anxious, restless, hungry, and have problems concentrating.[31] Smokers crave cigarettes and this makes them feel stressed. When they have their next cigarette, the craving goes away. They mistake this for relief, when really, the addiction is what causes the stress in the first place. [32]

POOR SPORTS PERFORMANCE

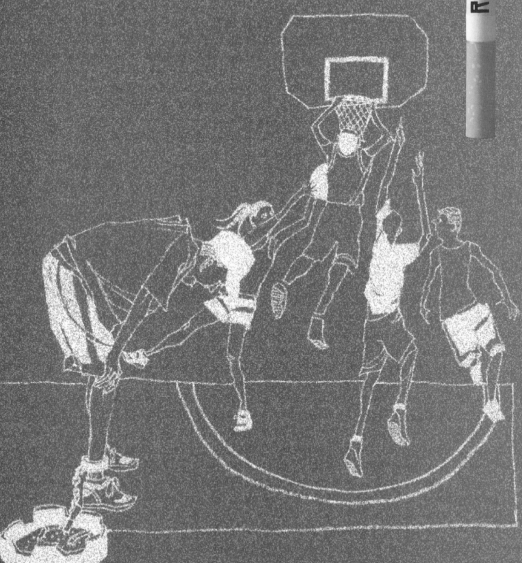

Kyle Young, 10

If there's one thing Kyle Young can't get enough of, it's football. He loves to watch the game, especially when his favorite team – the Atlanta Falcons – is on the field. But more than anything, Kyle loves to *play* football. One of his favorite memories is scoring his first touchdown in a football game when he was just six years old. "My dad got me into the sport when I was little," he says. Kyle started football when he was five years old, which means he's been playing for half of his life. He knows what it takes to succeed. "Don't ever smoke," is one main piece of advice Kyle has for kids who want to play sports. "And be sure to eat veggies," he adds.

Smoking is something he won't ever do because he knows how bad it is – especially when it comes to sports. "If you play sports and smoke, when you're trying to run, it will get hard to breathe," he explains.

Kyle knows that smoking would only get in the way of his dreams of playing football. His favorite position is quarterback, and he hopes to play professionally when he gets older. As Kyle explains, cigarettes are especially bad for athletes, which is why *this* future pro-football player will always take a pass on cigarettes and remain smoke-free.

DID YOU KNOW?

Some schools are performing mandatory testing for drugs (including nicotine) among their athletes. Players need to be clear of nicotine in order to pass the test and play. If members of these teams smoke, they won't be allowed in the game at all.[1]

In Kyle's own words ...

Smoking and Sports Don't Match

We have all heard that smoking is very bad for us. It can have an effect on everything we do. Everyone has a different reason why they choose not to take up smoking. My reason is that I play football. I do not want to lose out on all the hard work and time that I have put in to become good at football by doing something as stupid as taking up smoking.

It is important to take care of yourself and stay healthy, but when you are involved in sports it is even more important. You need to eat well, do lots of exercise, and get a good night sleep. If you are an athlete, no matter how well you take care of yourself, if you start smoking, it can ruin your career.

When athletes smoke, their sports performance suffers because of the carbon monoxide, nicotine, and the tar that is found in cigarettes. When you smoke, carbon monoxide causes your respiratory tract to swell. This stops the oxygen from circulating through your body. This makes your heart have to work harder. The muscles in our bodies can't work properly when they do not get enough oxygen. The carbon monoxide can also affect your eyesight. Nicotine in cigarettes causes your blood pressure to rise. It also gives you an increased heart rate. The tar causes your lungs not to work properly so you cannot breathe in enough air.

Smoking has a big effect on everyone, but athletes who smoke can no longer perform like they used to. Athletes who smoke are going to get tired faster – they won't be able to keep up at their practices and their games. They will be out of breath faster, and they will be much slower at whatever they do. This is why you don't see professional athletes smoking on the sidelines.

It is also why you don't see cigarette companies being allowed to support sporting events anymore.

If people are really into sports and stay active on a regular basis, they will probably not decide to take up smoking. The reason is because they don't want to ruin their chances of becoming better at their sport, and the kids they hang around with from their team probably feel the same way.

I think that all schools should try to keep kids active in sports. Schools should offer different kinds of activities so everyone can find something they like.

I know that I will never start smoking because I am 10 years old and I have been playing football for almost five years. I am really fast and I would never want to lose that. My dream is to become a professional football player, and I will not let smoking get in the way of my dreams.

DID YOU KNOW?

Troy Aikman, former Dallas Cowboys quarterback, and retired quarterback Steve Young have appeared on posters that urge fans not to use **spit tobacco** or drugs.[2] In the world of basketball, the Phoenix SUNS are saying no to tobacco as a team. SUNS guard Steve Nash says, "I've never been a smoker. My mom always told me it was really bad for you, that it could kill you. I've never tried a cigarette to this day." SUNS center Kurt Thomas says, "You can't smoke if you want to be an athlete. If you're out there trying to pursue a career in basketball, you're always gonna want to keep your lungs as clear as possible. Especially when playing with a guy like Steve Nash."[3]

Javier Lopez, catcher for the Atlanta Braves, John Smoltz, Atlanta Braves pitcher, Andres Galarraga, former Braves first baseman, and Derek Jeter, New York Yankees shortstop, all appear on posters that let young athletes know that all-stars don't need tobacco. Sammy Sosa's Centers for Disease Control and Prevention poster reads, "Sports and Tobacco Don't Mix – Be a Winner, Work Hard … Be Tobacco Free."[4]

INSTANT HISTORY FACTS

Baseball has been linked to tobacco since the National League started in 1876.[5] Players began to appear on trading cards that were included in cigarette packs only a few years later. As a scheme by tobacco companies to sell more cigarettes to fans, the cards usually had a picture of the player on the front and an ad for the tobacco company on the back.[6] Baseball players were known for using **spit tobacco**, also called **smokeless tobacco**, which comes in three forms: **chewing tobacco**, **moist snuff**, and **dry snuff**. Chewing tobacco comes in a leafy form or "plug" (which is tobacco that is pressed into the shape of a brick and is put right inside the cheek).[7] Users of chewing tobacco and moist snuff suck on a pinch of tobacco and spit out the excess saliva in big brown globs.[8]

Spit tobacco, partly because it doesn't release any smoke, was often mistakenly thought of as safer than cigarettes, but it's disfiguring and fatal results could not be ignored when tobacco started to take valuable athletes right out of the game. A US Department of Health report in 1986 showed that spit tobacco, like cigarettes, causes cancer.[9] Snuff and chewing tobacco increase the chances of getting **oral cancer**, which includes cancer of the lip, tongue, cheeks, gums, and the floor and roof of the mouth. Spit tobacco contains 28 **cancer-causing agents**, including arsenic, formaldehyde (fluid used to embalm corpses), and polonium-210 (nuclear waste).[10] Spit tobacco can also cause nicotine addiction.[11]

DID YOU KNOW?

Tons of athletes are sharing their incredible stories and strong opinions about the disastrous effects that tobacco has on the body and the ability to play sports. Rick Bender, a semi-pro ball player, lost a third of his tongue, half of his jaw, and all of the flesh connecting the right side of his neck to the rest of his body when he was in his 20s. This all happened as a result of chewing tobacco. He doesn't want young athletes to fall into the trap that he did – the one that tells you that tobacco is just part of the game. "Don't do what I did... don't believe them... don't wind up looking like I do," he says.[12]

Isaac A. Mastalski, 11

Isaac has a busy schedule, and although he is always on the go, he seems to have no problems keeping up. Some of this fifth grader's favorite activities include taking viola lessons and playing in the school band, swimming, playing basketball, and reading mystery and science fiction books. Isaac is also involved in Little League baseball, and it was his dedication to the sport, along with his feelings about tobacco, that led him to become the 2005 winner of the National Spit Tobacco Education Program's slogan contest. Isaac's winning slogan was "Use Spit Tobacco – You lose the game!" for which he won a trip to the Little League World Series. He was awarded a Louisville Slugger baseball bat at one of the games, but he says that the best part of the trip was handing out pins with his slogan on them. If that weren't enough, Isaac was also recently named one of the grand prize winners of an art contest. For someone this talented and ambitious, there is no place for tobacco!

Isaac thinks it's sad that baseball players use spit, or chewing tobacco, because he says that "a lot of Little League players look up to them, so kids might be getting the wrong idea about that kind of stuff." He also wishes that chewing tobacco were banned from professional baseball, but thinks that it might be hard because so many people do it. Inspired by the famous baseball poem "Casey at the Bat," Isaac decided to make a statement about smoking through verse. Isaac would never try tobacco in any of its forms because he says that it "damages your health and gives you a bad personal appearance." If he knew someone who was thinking about trying smoking or chewing tobacco, he would tell them that "it is a bad idea, because it could affect you physically, mentally, and even socially." As Isaac says, wouldn't you be "turned off of someone with yellow teeth or bad breath?"

 In Isaac's own words ...

"Yer Out!"

It was two-one in the last inning.
The air was thick with patience thinning.
There were two outs with a man on third.
Then Johnny was up, and groans were heard.
He was at bat and started to cough.
The crowd in the stands began to scoff.

Johnny had smoked and chewed for ten years,
Which gave him trouble hitting the spheres.
His teeth were yellowed; so was his skin.
Tobacco juice dribbled down his chin.

Everyone thought, "What good's a hitter,
Who is a smoker and a spitter?"
He used to hit far, impressed the crowd.
To autograph seekers his breath's loud.
Bam! The pitch was coming; what a gun!
He swung too late; the call was strike one.

From the mound the dirty brown dust rose.
Johnny's wrinkled yellowed hands just froze.
The pitch was good – "Strike two," roared the ump!
John's bad habits left him in a slump.

He wiped his brow and settled his hat,
Took one more practice swing of his bat.
He spat once more and stepped in the box.
He eyed the crowd – what a paradox!
From a distance they chanted his name
Ready to add this win to his fame.

He coughed; the pitcher released the ball.
It whizzed 'cross the plate – a mean curveball.
The umpire jumped, anxious to shout
Four sad little words – "Strike three! Yer out!"

ACTIVIST MOMENTS

Bill Tuttle started to chew tobacco when he joined the Major Leagues. As an outfielder for the Detroit Tigers, the Kansas City Athletics, and the Minnesota Twins, the photograph on his cards often showed a wad of chew tobacco in his cheek. Tuttle joined the battle against smokeless tobacco when he was diagnosed with **oral cancer**. Where he had once held a wad of chewing tobacco in his cheek, there was now a tumor that had to be removed. Surgery to take out the cancerous tumor also caused him to lose his jawbone, right cheekbone, and many of his teeth. Tobacco had stolen his face. In addition, he could no longer taste food. Tuttle told his story to other players. He also organized a program to test players for oral cancer. One hundred and forty one players volunteered to be tested in 1997, and 83 of them had oral **lesions**. While improving the lives of others, he was suffering from the effects of his disease. In 1998 he died of oral cancer.

Former baseball star and commentator Joe Garagiola carried on Tuttle's mission to educate players about the dark reality of smokeless tobacco and to prevent its use by acting as chairman of the National Spit Tobacco Education Program (NSTEP). NSTEP also worked with former Houston Astros player Jeff Bagwell to help spread the word. Bagwell was only 25 when leukoplakia (white leathery sores resulting from the smokeless tobacco juices that Bagwell had been sucking on) was found in his mouth. Bagwell's lesions developed very quickly, and he was surprised that this had happened to him while he was so young. Bagwell quit tobacco before the lesions spread and became cancerous. After he quit chewing tobacco, his batting average improved from .273 (in 1992) to .320 (in 1993). He was named the National League's Most Valuable Player in 1994.[13]

SMOKING STATS

Most spit tobacco users start the habit around age nine or ten.[14] Kids who use smokeless tobacco will likely start to smoke cigarettes too, which means that they are taking in a lot of nicotine. This not only makes it harder to breathe and harder to keep playing sports for long periods of time, but it can also cause athletes to get nervous and anxious – something you definitely don't want to be when you're in the game.[15] Young adults who smoke may think that they are healthy, but smoking makes the heart work so hard that it doesn't get to relax between beats, and this can lead to serious **heart dysfunction.**[16]

FAST FACTS

High school seniors who begin smoking by grade nine are twice as likely to report poorer overall health than nonsmokers – this means coughing up phlegm and blood, being short of breath even when they're not exercising, and wheezing and gasping. They are also absent from school more often than nonsmokers.[17]

FAST FACTS

People who smoke usually can't compete in sports with their nonsmoking peers because of the rapid heartbeat (which is increased by two to three beats every minute),[18] decreased **circulation***, and shortness of breath that occurs as a result of smoking.[19] Nicotine also squeezes the blood vessels, which can slow down reaction time and cause dizziness.[20] This can be a big problem if you need to stay steady to make a basket.*

In the words of Jill Schutjer's class ...
(See page 75 for more information about Jill Schutjer's class.)

Garrett Asmus, 12

If you chose to smoke, you will become non-active. Some examples are if you work on a farm, you might always drive, not walk, and you will have to buy more gas. If you have children and they want to play outside, you won't be able to play as long before you get tired. And if you don't exercise, you might get a round belly.

Haley Engelbarts, 13

If you want to be in sports, I suggest you don't start smoking. According to www.teengrowth.com, when you smoke, you don't have the energy to run or be active. If you are a smoker and play sports, you might have to tell your coach you have to go to the bathroom to take a smoke. You will not be able to run faster than your teammates and your opponents.

FAST FACTS

Smoking affects the ability to play sports in a number of ways. First of all, teen smokers are more likely than nonsmokers to suffer from **asthma** *and to have trouble breathing.[21] The lungs can't take in as much air, and shortness of breath can destroy an athlete's endurance.[22] A smoker's endurance is much lower than a nonsmoker's.[23] If you do 10 jumping jacks and then breathe through a straw, you'll see how hard it is to breathe when you're suffering from asthma. If you hold your breath for 30 seconds, you will feel how a smoker feels after running the length of a soccer field.[24]*

Haley Krull, 13

One reason not to start smoking is if you want to be an athlete. In sports, you will lose a large amount of energy. Smoking will slow you down by making you cough excessively. When you exercise, you will get extremely tired and out of breath. Smoking to me, as an athlete, wouldn't work. I want to be in any sport I can and excel greatly. But I can't have smoking hold me back.

Taylor Thomsen, 13

If you love sports, you shouldn't smoke. Smoking will just make it harder to breathe. So if you like football, you run a lot in football. You will be out of breath right away. School is when you try all the sports for the first time. If you smoke, you won't want to try them because you will be out of breath.

INSTANT HISTORY FACTS

In 2006, the Little League Baseball World Series set an example for the Major Leagues by banning tobacco on the field and in the stands in order to keep the players and fans healthy and ready for the game.[25]

Adam Michelin, 12

Adam Michelin has played defense in hockey since he was six years old. He likes the game so much that he plays street hockey in the summer and loves hockey video games – especially NHL 7 – when he can't get to the rink or play outside. Knowing just how much effort and dedication sports take, Adam can't imagine introducing cigarettes to the mix. "If you play sports and/or do any drugs, your sports career is ruined," he says. "Smoking can be the end of the world. Don't be fooled by the story I wrote because Ryan gets away with smoking. He could have died from cancer or other illnesses, and so can you if you smoke. You might never heal like Ryan did. If you ever have the urge to start smoking, slap yourself and ask why you ever wanted to smoke." It's clear that this hockey player and budding creative writer will never be game for tobacco.

DID YOU KNOW?

The chances of getting a sports-related injury may be two times higher for smokers than nonsmokers. Smokers take longer to heal because their bodies are slower in producing collagen, which helps treat injuries naturally.[26] In one study, smokers with fractures of the tibia (the lower leg bone) took four weeks longer to heal than nonsmokers with fractures.[27]

 In Adam's own words ...

Smoking Right Out Of Uniform

This is the story about Ryan and Jarome who both play hockey. Ryan is a tall, long-black-haired man whose hockey career is great. Jarome is a tall, short-black-haired man whose hockey career couldn't be better.

One night Ryan and Jarome are walking down a dark street when somebody grabs Ryan and Jarome, and pulls them into an alley. In the alley it was a mess. There were cigarettes and cigars all over the ground, along with needles for injecting drugs. One of the addicts offers them a cigarette. Ryan accepts but Jarome declines. For ten minutes Jarome tries to stop Ryan, but his efforts were futile. So Ryan tries a cigarette and gets addicted.

The next day, Ryan and Jarome were playing a hockey game. Ryan is a bit slower and a bit weaker. Jarome suspects something. The game ended in a tie because Ryan missed the winning goal and got yelled at by the coach. For the rest of the off-season Ryan kept smoking, making his lungs worse.

At the start of the regular season, Ryan had trouble just standing up, let alone playing. That's why they lost 10-0. When they were all alone, or so they thought, Jarome accused Ryan of smoking. Ryan admitted his guilt just as the coach jumped out. Ryan got caught and it was the worst day of his life. He got kicked off the team.

For the rest of the season Ryan tried to quit smoking, but his efforts were ineffective. He tried all summer and couldn't stop. Next season, he tried out for the team and barely made it. In the middle of his first game he passed out and got rushed to the hospital. It turned out he was so weak he couldn't walk or skate.

Two months pass and Ryan finally heals, deciding never to smoke again. Ryan made the right choice at the wrong time. Now Ryan could start feeling better, but he will never feel totally healthy. Next season, Ryan starts playing at his normal pace. He fixed his friendship with Jarome.

iNSTANT HiSTORY FACTS

- 1909 was an important year for tobacco-free sports, as Honus Wagner, shortstop for the Pittsburgh Pirates, demanded that his picture be taken off a set of baseball cards sold in cigarette packs. He is rumored to have done this because he was afraid that his picture on baseball cards would cause fans to smoke, and he did not approve of tobacco use. Since so few cards had been made before they were pulled from production, they became extremely rare. As a result, this particular card became one of the most valuable baseball cards of all time. Known as "The Holy Grail" of baseball cards, it is worth close to half a million dollars.[28]

- Between the 1920s and 1940s, both baseball and tobacco were booming, and the greats, including Babe Ruth, Joe DiMaggio, Ted Williams, and Lou Gehrig, were all featured in tobacco ads. In 1948, Babe Ruth, legendary starting pitcher for the Boston Red Sox and outfielder for the New York Yankees, died from oral cancer caused by tobacco and alcohol abuse. Ruth began chewing when he was around five years old and went on to own a cigar company. His use of tobacco and alcohol affected his performance on the field and made him weak. Later, he had trouble walking. At the 25th anniversary of Yankee stadium, Ruth, who had been the first player to ever hit 60 home runs in a season, walked onto the field using his bat as a cane.[29]

DID YOU KNOW?

Extreme sports athletes are totally into the tobacco-free movement too. Tony Hawk, pro skateboarder and extreme sports originator, has refused to let tobacco companies use his image to sell tobacco. He has also appeared on a poster for tobacco-free living. Athletes from a range of sports are featured in tobacco-free posters, including Olympic gold medalists Picabo Street (alpine skiing), Dominique Dawes (gymnastics), Brazilian soccer star Sissi, and World Cup champion mountain biker Alison Dunlap. Even Jackie Chan, martial arts master, has fought back against the tobacco industry in a "Strike Out Against Tobacco" poster.[30]

Micheala Philpitt, 11

Micheala wants to see professional athletes stop using tobacco because of the bad example they set for kids like her. She thinks that young people look up to their favorite sports stars and want to be just like them, even if it means smoking cigarettes or chewing tobacco. Micheala says that most kids probably start smoking because they think it will make them cool and popular. Seeing their idols smoke, she says, could push them even further to pick up the habit.

In Micheala's opinion, being involved in sports is one of the best ways to stay cigarette-free. She says that playing a sport could keep people from smoking because they would worry more about winning, and would want to stay healthy in order to play their best. Her favorite sport is soccer, and she knows that if she smoked, she wouldn't be able to keep up with the other players. If a smoker tried to be active, Micheala says, "They would feel horrible! They would be coughing a lot, their lungs would hurt, and it would probably slow them down. I don't think a smoker's heart would be as strong as the heart of a person who doesn't smoke." It is also important for Micheala to keep her mind in good shape. She has heard that nicotine can affect the way that your brain works when you play sports. "I use my brain to think about where the ball is going and to say stuff to the players and to concentrate on the game. Smoking can hurt that because it hurts your brain, so you'll have trouble thinking. You won't be able to focus and concentrate."

Micheala hopes that her words will help show people that when it comes to smoking, there are no winners, only losers, and that no one should play games with their health.

 In Micheala's own words ...

Eww! Smoking! Get away! It's bad for your health! This essay is about smoking and some of the effects it has on you. Here are all the things it can do to you. Smoking is bad for everyone. DO NOT let anyone force you into smoking. A good friend will not force you, but a bad friend would. Did you know that nine percent of eighth-graders smoke? Yet it is illegal for anyone under eighteen to do so!

Why exactly is smoking bad? Smoking is bad for a lot of reasons. It gives you upper respiratory and breathing problems. It gives you shortness of breath, dries out skin, causes wrinkles, makes your clothes and hair smell, turns your teeth and fingers yellow, gives you bad breath and makes you dehydrated. Smoking causes heart disease, more colds, and is the number one cause of lung cancer. Smoking is very addictive! Smoking affects your brain, lungs, heart, and liver, and your mouth and throat. Secondhand smoke is bad too.

Smoking affects everyone around you, not just yourself. It can even make people die that are around you. People around you will start to have problems with their insides too. It can make them cough, just as much as you. Or it can make them sick.

Smoking affects the way your body works. It can affect your ability to play sports. It will not allow you to exercise as much. Smoking affects your brain. You need your brain to play sports, but if your brain is affected, so is your ability to play sports. It will slow down your running ability, kicking ability, throwing ability, and hitting ability. Not getting enough exercise is going to make your body and muscles weaker. Smoking will help make you lazy. You would only want to smoke.

Now you know about smoking and what it can do to you. It is really bad. We should start a no-smoking policy. It is bad for everyone. People who smoke should stop. If they read this, they might realize what it is doing to them and hopefully stop. If they can't, they should try using gum to help stop smoking. If they still can't, at least stop polluting the cities with those disgusting cigarettes. DO NOT SMOKE!!!

ACTIVIST MOMENTS

Spit tobacco and cigarette use are a serious hurdle for athletes of any sport. The Smoke-Free Soccer program, created with the purpose of spreading tobacco-free messages around the world, has featured soccer stars from the US, Australia, Brazil, China, and Canada on their posters. Washington State (in the US) has a Tobacco-Free Team Program for soccer teams in Washington.[31] Tobacco-Free Sports in British Columbia, Canada, works to educate people about the negative effects of tobacco and the resulting decrease in sports performance. Tobacco-Free Sports is working to make the 2010 Olympics in British Columbia smoke-free so that the athletes can perform at their best.[32] Find out what programs your team can be a part of and then join in!

APPEARANCE

Brenna MacAulay, 9

Today, almost everyone knows that smoking is bad for your health, but not everyone thinks about just how smoking affects the way you look. Brenna is nine years old and she knows that if she smoked, she would soon look older. Many people only think about the long-term effects of smoking and think that the habit makes them look more mature, but Brenna realizes that cigarettes can give you wrinkles way before your time. She thinks that if people saw someone holding a cigarette, they might think twice about being their friend. Brenna might still be friends with someone who smokes, but says that she probably wouldn't spend as much time with them. Being exposed to secondhand smoke could hurt her health and appearance, and since Brenna is happy with the way she feels and looks, she wouldn't want to change for the worse because of cigarettes.

Looking and feeling her best counts when Brenna competes in gymnastics, and keeping her sense of taste is also important to her. She knows that if she smoked, she wouldn't enjoy her favorite foods as much – especially chocolate! – since smoking also damages your taste buds. Brenna decided that it was important for her to write this essay to let others know how bad smoking is for you, both inside and out. She has many role models among her friends and family who don't smoke, including her older sister, Lauren, who also feels strongly about exposing the ugly underside of cigarettes. (Read Lauren's opinions on smoking and entertainment on page 128.)

FAST FACTS

Tobacco smoke harms the skin in lots of ways. First off, the smoke in the environment dries the surface of the skin. Smoke also squeezes blood vessels so that there isn't as much blood flowing to the skin. This strips skin of oxygen and essential nutrients. Smoke turns the skin yellow and grey even when you're young, and can make it look leathery.[1]

 In Brenna's own words ...

Smoking and Body Image

If you think you want to start smoking, you should think again! Because if you like the way you look now, that can all change when you start smoking. When you smoke, the tar in the cigarettes will stain your teeth and fingers yellow. Smokers also have really bad breath! Also, when you smoke you will get wrinkles a lot earlier, especially on your face.

Are you happy with your hair the way it is? Did you know that you can lose some of it when you smoke? Do you like the taste of chocolate with a yummy caramel middle and maybe three different kinds of chocolate? I know I do. If you are a smoker, you won't be able to taste that yummy, gooey chocolate very well because smoking changes your ability to taste foods. Your clothes and hair will always smell like smoke. People who smoke and have acne (pimples) will have a harder time clearing up their skin than nonsmokers.

When you smoke you may think it's cool, but lots of other people won't! People who see you smoking might think you're bad or not nice just because you smoke. Your friends may not want to go over to your house because it smells bad. There are no good reasons that I can find to start smoking!

Now that I know all the things that can happen to my body, I don't think I would want to change my appearance just to have a cigarette … would you?

FAST FACTS

Puckering your lips around a cigarette can cause wrinkles around the mouth, and squinting from smoke can cause wrinkles around the eyes (these wrinkles around the eyes are called "crow's-feet"). [2]

INSTANT HISTORY FACTS

Smoking has long been known to cause wrinkles. In 1991, a study from the University of Utah Health Sciences Center was the first to show that smoking causes wrinkles on the face, even if you aren't often exposed to the sun. However, spending an hour in the sun every day, along with heavy smoking, greatly increases the risk of premature wrinkling (wrinkling way before you should be).[3] And in 2007, a study showed that smoking causes wrinkles not only on the face, but *all over* the body.[4]

DID YOU KNOW?

Psoriasis, a condition that makes the skin itchy and red, has been found to be twice as likely to develop in smokers than non-smokers.[5] Psoriasis causes dry, silvery scales on the skin – and these patches of itchy skin spread rapidly over the body, to the legs, back, elbows, and even the tongue.[6] Not only is psoriasis uncomfortable, it is a chronic condition, which means that it will never go away.

Palmoplantar Pustular Psoriasis (PPP) is a form of psoriasis that is often seen in smokers.[7] PPP causes little blisters filled with fluid to appear on the palms of the hand and the bottoms of the feet. After the pus oozes out, the blisters turn brown and scaly.[8]

ACTIVIST MOMENTS

Many beautiful women want to speak out about smoking.
For example:

- Model Christy Turlington is turning the "smoking is glamorous" myth upside-down by saying that "smoking is ugly." Christy began smoking when she was 13 but quit when her dad got lung cancer. After her dad passed away from cancer, she became an activist, joining forces with the Centers for Disease Control and Prevention. In 2000, she produced and hosted *Seven Deadly Myths*, a film that squashes common beliefs about smoking. She also appeared in a 2001 film called *Scene Smoking: Cigarettes, Cinema & the Myth of Cool*. Christy completely disagrees with the image of the "cool" smoker: "There is a strange sort of rebelliousness that is associated with smoking, and the thing is, it's such a false rebelliousness," she says. "There's nothing cool about it. It's conformity in the worst way."[9]

- Model Tyra Banks co-hosted "Smoking: The Truth Unfiltered," an episode of PBS's *In the Mix*. In the show, Tyra talks about the negative physical effects of tobacco that seriously impact smokers *right now* – not just when they're older. Tyra says that she can't understand why people would smoke. "I, for one, have not smoked and I don't understand why they do it, because smoking yellows your teeth and nails," Tyra says. "It makes your skin all sallow and wrinkly and it gives you dull hair. You know, those models out there that do smoke are contributing to this image that, if you do smoke, you'll be beautiful, you'll be popular, and it's totally not true."[10]

- Susan Sarandon responded to fellow actress Kristen Dunst's inquiry as to why Susan's skin looked so good by pointing out the importance of not smoking: "Well, first off, don't smoke... I do see the difference between people of my age who have smoked all their lives and those who haven't."[11]

In the words of Jill Schutjer's class ...

(See page 75 for more information about Jill Schutjer's class.)

Anna Skarpohl-Ost, 13

Smoking can wreck your appearance. Your teeth get yellow, your fingertips get yellow, and your skin can get wrinkly. Your skin can also get really pale. Do you want to look like you are dressed up for Halloween everyday? I bet not. You will probably smell if you smoke. If you are looking for a job of any kind, people won't want you because you smell bad. They are probably looking for a cleaner person. Smoking can really wreck how you look and smell. Your outside doesn't look good and neither do your lungs and heart. They turn black. GROSS! I bet you don't want to look and feel bad the rest of your life. You want to have money for stuff you want and for your bills; you want to look good and feel good, don't you? Be smart, use your brain, and do not start smoking!

Jared Irons, 13

Smoking can affect your appearance, and it can affect your smell. Even if you smoke just once, you will smell terrible. Your teeth also turn yellow and it looks nasty. I don't think that you would want your teeth to look like a banana peel.

Sara Christians, 12

Smoking can change your appearance. It will make your teeth yellow and rotted. It will make you and your possessions reek. It will make your hair thin out and it will get all oily. It will make your face break out. Smoking will change who you are. These are some of the ways it can change your appearance.

Jessica Kirk, 13

Smoking can affect the way you look. Your nails might have a yellow tint to them, and your teeth will probably be yellow no matter how many times you brush them. They might even fall out – gross! Your appearance can make people uncomfortable around you, and they might get up and leave you all alone smoking your cigarette. Is that what you're willing to pay for if you start smoking? Also, your lungs will turn black from being unhealthy, and you won't be able to run or do the things you want, like playing football or going out for a sport, because you'll be gasping for breath the whole time. Which sounds better: being able to run and play or sitting alone smoking? I don't know about you, but I'd choose running and playing. Wouldn't you?

Maranda Eichenberger, 13

Smoking always takes a toll on how you look and smell. You carry the smell of smoke in your breath and clothes. Your teeth turn an icky yellowish color. Your gums turn blackish. Your face can become wrinkly at a younger age than a nonsmoker's, and smoking can increase your chances of getting some kinds of skin diseases. Smokers tend to get more visible wrinkles around their eyes and mouth. In fact, smokers in their forties have as many wrinkles as a person in their sixties who does not smoke. Your nails start to turn an icky yellowish brown color, especially in the hand you hold your cigarette. You don't look healthy and your appearance is not pretty if you start smoking.

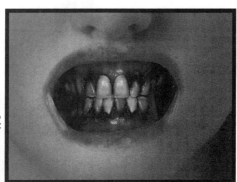

A picture-based health warning that appears on cigarette packages in Canada.

FAST FACTS

If you smoke, you can lose your teeth early. Researchers have found that smokers are up to six times more likely to develop gum disease than nonsmokers, and this causes the gums to shrink away from the teeth. It also causes the destruction of the bone that holds teeth in place, so the teeth can fall out.[12]

 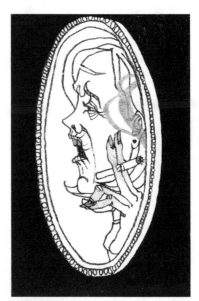

SMOKING STATS

Smoking may double your chances of suffering from Age-related Macular Degeneration (AMD) — an eye disorder that is the leading cause of blindness in the US. In some cases, it can cause the eyes to bleed.[13] And the more you smoke, the more likely it is that you'll develop **cataracts**. Cataracts can cause blindness.[14] So not only do smokers find an unpleasant surprise when they look in the mirror, but they may not be able to see anything at all.

DID YOU KNOW?

In 2003, the Task Force for Tobacco-Free Women and Girls in New York State invented a computer software program that shows how smoking affects the way a smoker's face looks. The program used images that were created from photographs of 2,000 real smokers and nonsmokers. The Task Force made presentations to middle schools and high schools, taking photographs of participants and running the photographs through the program. In only five minutes, participants can see what their faces will look like 30 years from now if they start smoking when they are young.[15] This invention became the first version of APRIL© Age Progression Software, which is still being used and has helped to show that someone who smokes a pack of cigarettes every day will have as many wrinkles as a nonsmoker 1.4 times older. So a 20-year-old smoker would look like a 28-year-old who doesn't smoke.[16]

SMOKING STATS

Less than 5% of young people in the Bahamas, Barbados, Costa Rica, Indonesia, Malawi, Montserrat, Poland, Russia, Singapore, Ukraine, and Venezuela think girls who smoke look more attractive.[17]

Jessica Brisebois, 13

To Jessica, smoking is a disgusting habit, which is why it makes her cringe whenever she sees teenagers walking down the street with cigarettes in their hands. Teachers and nurses have taught her and her classmates about the long-term health effects of smoking, but Jessica has already witnessed the damage that smoking can do in the short-term. She knows that smoking can change your appearance quickly, and seeing kids at school with their hands and teeth stained yellow from nicotine is enough to prove it.

Although Jessica believes that most people her age are aware of the risks, she says that some still choose to smoke because they want to be rebellious. They may not think that cigarettes are a big deal, but Jessica does. She knows that in addition to hurting your health and changing your appearance, smoking affects how others might perceive you. She believes that smoking can give the wrong impression of the kind of person someone is on the inside, and people may not go out of their way to get to know someone if he or she is surrounded by a cloud of smoke.

While some think that smoking makes them look cool, Jessica wrote this essay to remind people that smokers are in the minority, and that a cigarette is not – and won't ever be – a fashionable accessory.

In Jessica's own words ...

"Cigarettes?" It's one of the most frequently asked questions in school. "Where are they?" "Want a smoke?" Teachers always remind us of what happens to your lungs when you smoke, but they never talk about physical appearance. Your physical appearance is very affected when you smoke. Personally I think it can cause pimples. Most people I know that smoke have pimples. Pimples aren't a very pretty thing. So then why do people do things that cause them? That is a question I am still trying to figure out. I also notice that people who smoke have yellow hands. I think appearance isn't only your skin. I find if I see a teenager smoking, it looks bad. Having a cigarette between your fingers and just standing there makes people look trashy. I know that might sound a little mean, but it is the truth.

One thing I can say is that our society has come a long way from the older times. Back then everyone used to smoke. Doctors, actors, almost everyone. In the 1970s and 1980s they didn't have the knowledge that we have now. They didn't think it was a big deal. Everyone in movies used to smoke, which would influence more people to smoke. Nowadays, they have famous actors doing commercials on anti-smoking. They are trying to influence us not to smoke.

So if someone asks me what I think about smoking my answer is always going to be the same. Smoking is disgusting. It's a waste of money. Cigarettes are killers. We should be doing everything in our power to stop people from smoking. The less smoking, the cleaner the air.

FAST FACTS

The tar in tobacco smoke turns smokers' fingers yellow and stains their fingernails. The fingers and fingernails on the hand that holds the cigarette have the worst stains.[18]

DID YOU KNOW?

Even smokers' hair is affected by their bad habit. Smokers' blood carries deadly chemicals and gases that affect the body's red blood cells, which means that the cells can no longer carry the right amount of oxygen throughout the body. As a result, the hair does not get enough nutrients or oxygen from the bloodstream, which makes the top layers of the hair brittle.[19] Smoking can also cause both male and female smokers to lose their hair, which means that smokers can go bald early.

SMOKING STATS

- Smoking puts so much stress on your heart that smoking one pack of cigarettes a day is the equivalent of your body functioning as if it were 90 pounds overweight.[20]

FAST FACTS

- Smoking can cause fat to be stored irregularly, which can cause serious health problems. Smoking affects the shape of the body because fat is stored around the waist or upper torso instead of around the hips. This is dangerous because it leads to an increased risk of developing **diabetes**, **heart disease**, **high blood pressure**, **gallbladder problems**, and breast and uterine cancer in females.[21]

- In 2007, one study showed that although girls are smoking because they think that it will help them control their weight, smoking doesn't do this at all; whether they smoke or not, girls gain weight at the same rate. Girls are being told by **Big Tobacco** that they will lose weight if they smoke, but now we know that this is not true. The study also found that guys who smoked were shorter than guys who didn't smoke, and that smoking may stunt their growth if they take up the habit before they hit puberty. [22]

THE ENTERTAINMENT TRAP

Steffani Brass Vaughn, 15

Breaking into show business is super hard to do. Some actors and actresses work for years before they get their first job, but 15-year-old Steffani Brass managed to get her start in the industry early – *very early*. She was only four years old when she first started working! Since then, this talented California girl has been in a ton of movies and TV shows, including *That 70s Show, Friends, Gilmore Girls, The Amanda Show,* and *Malcolm in the Middle.* In addition to all of the TV shows and movies she has worked on, Steffani has also found the time to talk about cigarettes in movies and on TV. In her essay on smoking and the entertainment industry, Steffani explains why she chooses to stay away from cigarettes, and why it's a problem when young people see other actors and actresses smoking on screen. Like any high school student, Steffani wants to do well in school and also have fun. She knows that smoking won't help her accomplish either of those things. As she says, smoking isn't fun, it won't make her any cooler, it won't help her make friends, and it definitely won't help her do well in school or at work. These are just some of the reasons why Steffani chooses not to smoke. Now *this* is an entertainer to watch!

In Steffani's own words ...

Smoking and the Entertainment Industry - It Shouldn't Connect

As a 15-year-old girl who attends high school and also works as an actress, the one thing I try to do is stay on the straight and narrow. As hard as it is not to fall into "following the crowd," the one thing I will never follow is smoking.

To me, smoking is the most disgusting thing a person can do. Not only can it cause cancer, but it smells awful. There's nothing more disgusting than being somewhere and a person walks by who is not smoking, but I can tell right away that they've been smoking because they smell.

Being an actress and working a lot in the entertainment field, I have been around a lot of adults and I've probably worked with more adults than kids. I can only remember one adult actor constantly taking a cigarette break. I was nine years old and I remember saying to my mother, "Ew ... he smokes, Mom." It really bothered me. I'm sure there were others, but I never noticed them. I guess it's because he did it so frequently.

Because I started acting when I was four, I never had to worry about getting parts that needed me to smoke. Now that I'm a teenager, I know that someday it might come up. The problem with showing teens smoking in the movies is that it makes it seem like it's okay to smoke if you're watching your favorite actor/actress smoke on the screen. There are still many kids that are constantly trying to be "cool" and unfortunately, smoking cigarettes is one of the things that they think can still make them look cool. What they don't realize is that they don't look cool – they just look stupid. When I watch a movie and it's about kids who do drugs or drink, they always have the kids with cigarettes. The only good thing about that is that it shows me that if I ended up getting into drugs and drinking, I would probably also be smoking. It just shows the negative picture of that whole sad problem and it definitely keeps me from ever wanting to get into that kind of lifestyle.

I don't think they need to have any actor smoke in movies or TV. It doesn't make sense to me. What's the point in telling your audience that it's okay to smoke and get cancer? What's the point in using a cigarette, even as a prop? If producers are making a film that takes place in the days when smoking was okay and no one knew how bad it is for you, then I still believe that they don't have to have the actors smoke. The movie isn't about smoking. The shows aren't about smoking. A story can be told to anyone without anyone having to smoke a cigarette unless it's crucial to the storyline. As I mentioned before, drugs = drinking = cigarettes.

I'm glad I don't have the need to feel like I have to do something to be part of a crowd. Be your own person and stick up for what you believe in. Smoking is a horrible habit. It's addictive, it smells, it lingers, and it causes cancer.

ACTIVIST MOMENTS

After being pressured by citizens, numerous organizations, and 32 state attorneys who all asked for tougher ratings on movies containing smoking, the Motion Picture Association of America (MPAA) has said that it will consider how a movie portrays smoking when they decide on what rating it should have. If a movie is given a stricter rating because it glamorizes smoking, then the fact that it glamorizes smoking will be included in the description of the movie for all to see.[1] The MPAA does not automatically give a movie an R rating because there is smoking in it, in part because they do not want to **censor** movies, but this small step may help to make the public more aware of what they are seeing, and let the movie studios know that glamorizing smoking is not okay.[2]

If you think that smoking and movies shouldn't mix, there are things that you can do right from your own computer. Go to www.smokefreemovies.ucsf.edu to find out how to contact Hollywood's major studios, and ask them to become the first studio that does not allow smoking in films targeted at young viewers.

DID YOU KNOW?

Smoking may be everywhere in the movies, but many of the biggest celebrities today are speaking out against cigarettes. Jennifer Hudson, Oscar-winning *Dreamgirls* actress, makes her position clear: "I don't drink. I don't smoke."[3] In a *Barnes & Noble* interview, Natalie Portman said: "I don't think movies should glamorize smoking."[4] Kay Panabaker, who has starred in *Summerland, Phil of the Future,* and *CSI*, and plays George in *Nancy Drew* (2007), filmed an anti-smoking Public Service Announcement and was nominated for the Young Artist Award for Best Performance in a Commercial for Youth Anti-Smoking.

Television stars are also talking about smoking on the small screen. Adam Brody, who plays Seth on *The OC*, told *YM* about what happened when there was smoking in *The OC*: "...in the pilot, there was a scene where Ryan and Marissa (Mischa Barton) smoke. They have since gotten a lot of calls from parents, and they've taken it out – Ryan doesn't smoke anymore ..."[5]

INSTANT HISTORY FACTS

In black-and-white movies from the 1930s, 1940s, and 1950s, smoking was treated as a cool thing to do. Back then, before the 1964 US Surgeon General's report that linked smoking to early death, people didn't know that smoking was dangerous.

The strange thing is that even once smoking was known to cause health problems, movies still tried to make smoking look cool and glamorous. In 1971, tobacco commercials on TV became illegal in the United States[6], and big tobacco companies had figured out that movies with hip characters who smoked would be like advertisements for their cigarettes. The cigarette companies also thought that they could pay studios to include cigarettes in movies without the audience ever knowing that it was all part of their plan to get people to smoke.[7]

When *Superman II* was released in 1980, Lois Lane was shown on screen as a smoker even though she hadn't been a smoker in the comics. The tobacco company Philip Morris reportedly paid $42,000 to get the Marlboro brand logo in the movie. On screen, Lois Lane chain-smokes Marlboro Lights, and there are big Marlboro signs on the side of a van and on top of a taxi. One of Superman's fights is also staged with Marlboro billboards all around him.[8] This became a well-known example of a tobacco company paying a movie studio to place cigarettes in movies, but it is definitely not the only example. According to the American Legacy Foundation, the producers of *License to Kill*, a James Bond movie released in 1989, were paid $350,000 to make the James Bond character smoke Lark cigarettes.[9]

Tobacco companies also paid actors to smoke in films.[10] One company even set up a program that would give free cigarettes every month to actors who smoked in movies.[11] **The Master Settlement Agreement (MSA)** (1998) finally made it illegal for tobacco companies to pay actors or to get their brands in movies, music, and video games.[12] Despite this, smoking in the movies hasn't changed much since the 50s. In the 2002 movie *Men in Black II*, the aliens smoke Marlboros.[13] Tobacco companies are still getting cigarettes in movies by *donating* products with their logos on them, and because they are not *paying* the movie studios to do it, it is legal.

The 2005 movie *Thank You for Smoking*, a comedy about a Big Tobacco **lobbyist**, shows audiences how sneaky big tobacco executives can be, and how much they depend on the entertainment industry to convince people to start smoking. Though it does not take a strong anti-smoking position, it makes people think about the tobacco industry's role in movies, and has people talking about the subject.

DID YOU KNOW?

Tobacco companies have managed to find a way to get into the music business too! In 1997, Philip Morris created its own record label called "Woman Thing Music," which was named after the Virginia Slims ad campaign slogan, "It's a woman thing." Their albums, featuring new female performers, could only be purchased along with two packs of Virginia Slims cigarettes. This was seen as a move to get younger people who like pop music to buy smokes just so that they could get the CD.[14]

Lauren MacAulay, 12

Lauren doesn't believe everything that she sees on TV, and she thinks that celebrities often give kids the wrong idea about smoking, on the screen and off. She knows that featuring famous people smoking in movies, on television, and within the pages of fashion magazines sets a bad example for kids, who might think that they can be like their favorite stars if they choose to light up. Lauren is smart enough to know that what you see in Hollywood isn't always reality. Although fewer and fewer people are actually smoking in real life, she says that she probably sees smoking in movies or on TV at least a few times a week. Lauren also thinks that giving movies with smoking scenes an R-rating might force directors not to use cigarettes in their films, since fewer people will be able to go see them.

Seeing the way that the entertainment industry influences kids to smoke convinced Lauren to put her feelings on paper. She's challenging others not to let themselves be influenced by images of cigarettes that they see on the screen.

FAST FACTS

*Cool movies don't have to feature cigarettes. **The Devil Wears Prada** (2006), which is about the glamorous, high-stress world of the fashion magazine industry, doesn't show smoking at all.*[15]

 In Lauren's own words ...

Smoking in Entertainment

Smoking – it's all around us. Outside stores, in peoples' homes, at bus stops, and especially in entertainment. Chances are, if you've watched movies or TV lately, you've seen someone smoking. Smoking can also be heard about in music and seen in music videos. In the 1970s and 1980s everyone smoked. It was normal and no one knew of all the terrible dangers. Now it is well known that smoking is bad. So why does the entertainment business still show smoking?

In the entertainment business everything is very visual. Therefore, there are stereotypes people use that are meant to mean a certain thing, even if in reality it doesn't really mean that at all. One of these stereotypes is that people with glasses, a tucked-in shirt, buck teeth, etc., are meant to be "nerds" and losers. In reality, none of these things make you a nerd or a loser. Other stereotypes include: popular people are better looking than regular people; men are tougher than women (and are portrayed that way); and that tough/cool people smoke. Very often men and women are made to look popular, tough, rich, important and/or sexy by smoking. Again, like the other stereotypes, this one is very untrue! By putting smoking in movies, it is advertising. It is especially bad to put smoking in children's and teen movies, because these audiences are easily influenced and could be tempted to try it. This age group also looks up to many people: parents, teachers, and celebrities. Many young people want to be like the person they look up to and, if they see their favorite celebrities smoking in a movie, they could want to try it too. Therefore, it makes no sense why there should be smoking in movies. There are many ways of portraying a person as being popular, tough, rich, important, or cool without them smoking.

You may ask, "Why are people allowed to put smoking in movies?" or, "Why would I want to watch a movie where everyone is smoking?" Well, you may not want to watch the movie, but there are other people who don't care, don't mind, or who even like it. In fact, so many people are used to seeing or being around smoking that many times it goes unnoticed. Many movies, animated or not, for children or not, have only minor parts in which one or more characters smoke. By the time the movie is finished, people don't even remember that part. So why do they even need to put such a minor smoking part in the movie? They don't! In some movies, the character starts smoking to make them look more popular, or the character pictures themselves as more popular if they smoked. Some characters even take up smoking to impress people, and they are then shown as being liked more and being more popular once they start smoking. This gives the message that if you smoke, you will be popular and well-liked. All of these things are very untrue. Less often shown is someone who smokes and because they smoke people turn away and are against it. Hardly ever do you watch TV or a movie where a character smokes or takes up smoking and people react badly to it. That would bring across a much more realistic message. If there has to be smoking in a movie, wouldn't we all rather see the better message, the one against smoking? I know I would!

Will smoking in entertainment (and smoking period) ever be a thing of the past? Hopefully someday it will. Until then, strive not to be persuaded into smoking and strive to help do the same for others who are close to you. Who knows, maybe someday you will grow up and work in movies. If you do, before deciding to put smoking in your movie, ask yourself is it really worth it?? Together, as a society working to stop smoking, we say NO!

DID YOU KNOW?

The internet is playing a big part in shedding light on tobacco in the entertainment industry, and it is doing it in cool and fun ways. At OVX.org, the web site for the youth-led movement Our Voices Exposed (OVX), you can learn about the appearance of tobacco in movies and find out if you could be the next great filmmaker of the 21st century by creating your own movie. You can even email the site to your friends and challenge them to make a movie too. On another website, www.scenesmoking.org, you can see reviews for hot new films and find out if they get a rating of a pink lung or a black lung (pink lungs are for films without tobacco use, and black lungs are for films with tobacco use.)

ACTIVIST MOMENTS

One way to fight back against product placement (the placement of cigarette packages or brand logos in movies and TV shows) is to make anti-tobacco ads. The Florida Tobacco Control Program has run anti-tobacco ads in Florida movie theaters, on TV, and on billboards. They also have gone to schools with information about tobacco and the entertainment industry. Their tobacco education program ended up cutting down smoking rates in middle schools by 50% and high schools by 35%.[16] The American Cancer Society has also placed anti-smoking posters on the sets of television shows like *ER*. The next time you're watching TV, look to see if you can find one of the posters![17]

Shresht Lamba, 11

Shresht loves the movies because he can go with friends and family, get a big bucket of popcorn, and just relax while he watches a new flick. One thing Shresht doesn't like about movies is when they show people smoking cigarettes. What's the problem with actors and actresses smoking on screen? "It influences audiences," he explains. "When people see actors smoke, they think it's okay and don't realize how bad it is for you. Smoking is very bad for you. It can ruin a person's life or their family's life."

His favorite movie is *Mission Impossible 3*, which stars his favorite actor, Tom Cruise. One of the reasons he likes Tom Cruise so much, he explains, is that the star is never seen smoking in his films. "He sets a good example," Shresht says. "When actors smoke, it sets a bad example." Shresht is careful to point out that just

> **DID YOU KNOW?**
>
> Cigarette brands have also been advertised in video games. The old-school racing game *Pole Position II* (1983), and its sequel, *Atari Final Lap* (1987), both had virtual Marlboro billboards displayed along the tracks.[18]

because an actor smokes in a movie, it doesn't mean he smokes in real life. "In movies, everything you see isn't real. An actor could be smoking a plastic cigarette," he says. So just because you *see* somebody smoking in a movie, it doesn't mean that it's the real thing.

Whether they are smoking a real cigarette or not, Shresht doesn't like it when an actor or actress smokes in a movie. He's concerned about what smoking does to the health of viewers who smoke just because someone on the screen smokes. "I want to be healthy. I'd rather play basketball or soccer," he says. "Smoking is bad for you. Whether it's one or 100 cigarettes, it's still hurting your body." Shresht knows all about the harmful ingredients in just one cigarette. "They have tar and ingredients that are also in toilet bowl cleaner and gasoline." Shresht doesn't understand why any person would want to ruin his or her health by ingesting those kinds of things. "Don't people who smoke know what's going into your body? I mean, c'mon, it's like you're a toilet!" he exclaims.

Obviously, if you want to stay healthy, you should never start smoking. "You will have a longer, better life if you don't smoke," Shresht agrees. That is one of the reasons why Shresht has been trying to get his dad to quit. "My dad smokes, so it's a pretty personal issue for me. But now he's quitting," says Shresht, who is helping his dad kick his cigarette habit. Shresht realizes how addictive cigarettes are, and how hard it is to stop smoking once you've started. He is helping his dad by being supportive and by helping to keep track of how much his dad smokes. "He's down to one or two puffs," he says. Seeing how hard it has been for his dad to quit, Shresht doesn't understand why anybody would *ever* start smoking. "It ruins your life," he says. "Just because you see an actor smoke in a movie, that doesn't make it cool." He definitely knows that smoking is *not* cool, and he's not going to let a movie or actor change his mind about *that*. If he could have his way, smoking would never make the cut.

 In Shresht's own words ...

Showing silver screen characters smoking is a common feature. It seems a normal part of the script. Smoking doesn't bother anyone in the movies because it is on the screen only, but do you know what effect it's having on people who actually do smoke? Around the world, millions of people start smoking because they see it in the movies. Why do they want to smoke? There are a lot of other acts in movies – why don't they copy those acts, like dancing on the streets or making funny faces in front of the public? The audiences find actors smoking as a cool thing. The truth is that smoking is a bad habit and is harmful to the body and the environment.

Now, as people have noticed, smoking has become very popular and common in movies. Why? Why smoke? They have much better things they could show and at the same time not have such a bad influence on youngsters. The movie makers show characters smoking as part of normal life, but they should realize that the young audience gets attracted to it and that they are ruining their lives. Most smokers start at a young age to make themselves a part of the cool gang or as part of their cool style. Some smoke because their heroes smoke on the screen, or they find it a stress reliever.

We need to help put a stop to more people joining this death trap. It is a big mistake to smoke, and people who don't smoke can see that very well. Nonsmokers should help educate other people. There are a lot of steps that have been taken in the recent years by the governments, like putting a stop to smoking billboards, and stopping cigarette advertisements from being aired or printed in any form. Now it is time for us to add to the drive by advising our friends and relatives to quit smoking and by not adding ourselves to the list. In the end, if you still want to ruin your life, image, and lose friends, then please smoke all you want. If you want to keep your image and have friends, then don't smoke.

FAST FACTS

Smoking scenes in movies result in the purchase of so many cigarettes that American tobacco companies make about $4.1 billion US every year from movie appearances alone.[19] Smoking in movies is the most powerful influence on young viewers – even more powerful than magazine or billboard advertisements. Thirty-eight percent of teens in the US are estimated to have started smoking because of cigarettes in movies that they have seen. Those who watch many movies with smoking are nearly three times more likely to start smoking than those who watch few.[20]

In the movies, people who smoke often look rebellious, independent, young, good-looking, sexy, successful, and rich. In reality, people who smoke are not better looking or more successful, and they don't have more money. People may start to smoke to be just like a character in a movie, but it's all just an illusion.[21]

SMOKING STATS

The appearance of tobacco brands in films for teens *is* just as common as *it is* in films for adults. The brands are also *visible* in films for young children.[22] Studies have even found that PG-13 movies contain *more* tobacco use than R-rated films made for adults.[23] In 2004 and 2005, 68% of the top PG-13 movies contained smoking, which works out to over 14 incidents of smoking per hour.[24] Two out of three US live-action movies in 2006 featured tobacco.[25]

FALSE ADVERTISING

FALSE ADVERTISING

Jolie Yang, 17

When she was 13, Jolie attended her first anti-tobacco group meeting. These meetings have now become a part of her life. For the past four years, she has been a member of Asian American Youth Against Tobacco and has made it her mission to spread the word about **Big Tobacco**'s lies. Jolie recalls reading fashion magazines filled with tobacco ads when she was younger. At the time, she believed that by smoking, she could be cool like the stars shown with cigarettes between their fingers. Today, Jolie is much more aware of the truth behind tobacco advertising and of how tobacco companies use attractive but dishonest ads to get their products into the hands of young people like her.

Jolie's desire to connect with others who had similar experiences has pushed her to work toward making a difference beyond her community. Last year, she joined Ignite, an anti-tobacco group for young people who want to change tobacco laws across the nation. She even organized a chapter of Ignite in her area and has since been named National Secretary of the group. Jolie was also involved in getting a smoke-free ballot passed – a law that made smoking at work illegal in her state – and she is now working to make sure that people are taking this law seriously. The fight against tobacco has led her to different parts of the world – she has traveled to Taiwan twice to speak with people about the dangers of smoking. During her trip she conducted surveys to learn more about people's attitudes and beliefs about tobacco. In the future, she hopes to travel to China and India.

Jolie was recognized for her dedication to the cause when she was named International Youth Advocate of the Year by the Campaign for Tobacco-Free Kids. While in Washington to receive her award, Jolie got the chance to meet with two senators and a representative from her state. She also learned how to work with people on Capitol Hill in tackling smoking-related issues. Jolie plans to continue to be a leader in the anti-tobacco crusade and says that she wrote this essay to let people know that, "Big Tobacco kills, there are no health benefits to smoking, and it's not cool."

DID YOU KNOW?

Some cigarette advertising is easy to spot, like TV ads. Other advertising is sneakier. Tobacco companies sponsor contests and street festivals. By paying for an event to be named after their companies like this, the companies can display their logos and get their names out there. The fewer people smoking in the world, the more money companies spend on advertising in the hopes of attracting more customers.[1]

In Jolie's own words ...

The Fight Within

Making a closed peace sign, I held between my fingers a single straw, desperately wishing it were a cigarette. I had barely started elementary school, but I already knew all about tobacco, specifically cigarettes – at least I thought I did. I knew that older kids and adults were smoking; I knew that glamorous stars were smoking; but what I didn't know at that time was how harmful smoking could be. Enraptured by billboards, advertisements, and stars, I wanted to be "cool." I eventually grew out of my beginning stages of becoming a regular customer of **Big Tobacco**, and instead I became an activist encouraging youths to either stop smoking or to fight for political change on the subject. My childhood experiences encouraged me not to smoke and to take the message nationally and internationally.

My older sister Jessica joined an anti-tobacco group called Asian American Youth Against Tobacco (AAYAT) when I was in middle school, and she encouraged me to join as well. At first I was reluctant, but nevertheless I accompanied my sister in her weekly excursions to AAYAT meetings, and soon I became a happy companion. This change came from discovering and learning about the deceitfulness of Big Tobacco. I was horrified by how much leniency was granted to Big Tobacco by the government, allowing Big Tobacco to artfully use cigarettes in movies, glamorous ads in magazines, and huge ads barely three feet off the ground, all with the sole purpose of targeting kids and teenagers.

Incensed, I started to do a little research and discovered that Big Tobacco spends approximately $750 million on advertising in my state, while funding toward tobacco prevention programs such as AAYAT is being cut. I sincerely believe that the **Master Settlement Agreement**, which sprung anti-tobacco programs nationwide, caused a ripple effect, reducing the average number of smokers each year. It is because of the MSA that I was able to have the opportunity to join a local program like AAYAT, which ignited my passion to take my message nationally and internationally.

As the fight against Big Tobacco gains more momentum, I have started to encounter exasperated students and citizens who feel that the fight is an old fight, something that should either die down or be fought quietly and peacefully. What many do not realize is that Big Tobacco uses many discreet tactics in targeting people as restrictions on Big Tobacco increase. Furthermore, Big Tobacco is now starting to target many foreign countries, often targeting impoverished areas. Many citizens in foreign countries are not aware of the health effects and the tactics that Big Tobacco employs. I recently went to Taiwan, and many of the students there thought that there were only five ingredients in cigarettes and that secondhand smoke was not harmful. My experience in Taiwan showed that many countries do not have data and knowledge regarding Big Tobacco. Aside from the health effects, Big Tobacco's products result in child labor where many children are harmed by the harvesting and cultivation of tobacco. All of these instances prove how the fight against Big Tobacco still has a long way to go.

Being an advocate of fighting against Big Tobacco, I now focus on two different aspects of the fight: social change (educating youths) with AAYAT, and political change (**lobbying** issues) with Ignite. After years of being with AAYAT, joining Ignite helped raise my fight against tobacco to a whole new level. My personal experience as a victim of Big Tobacco's advertising motivates me to travel and educate youths, making sure they don't fall into the trap that I nearly did. That Big Tobacco often gets away with many issues while other companies don't always comes as a shock to me. This leniency also represents the long fight ahead before the movement against Big Tobacco wins, ultimately saving millions of lives.

DID YOU KNOW?

Tobacco companies do tons of research to find out what magazines you read, what TV channels you watch and what sports teams you cheer for. But you might not know that some tobacco companies are already in your kitchen cupboards. Philip Morris, the world's largest transnational tobacco company, owns many cigarette brands, including Marlboro, Players, Virginia Slims, and Chesterfield. They also own Kraft Foods, Nabisco and Christie, which make Kraft Dinner, Jell-O, Cool Whip, Post Cereal, Kool-Aid, Oscar Mayer, and Ritz Crackers. Check the packaging next time you eat one of these foods and you'll notice that they don't ever mention cigarettes. However, every time you buy Teddy Grahams or Oreos you are giving Philip Morris more money to make and advertise cigarettes.[2]

Meenakshi Malik, 11

If you ask Meenakshi what her favorite type of candy is, she doesn't hesitate: "I like gummy candies, especially Swedish Berries," she says without missing a beat. But sometimes when she's at the store to buy candy, Meenakshi notices something weird. "It bothers me how in some of the stores they put the candy right near the cigarettes," she says. Why? "It might make kids think about cigarettes and smoking because a lot of kids see the cigarettes while they are getting candy," she explains. "Sometimes the shiny cigarette packages even *look* like candy." Meenakshi has also noticed that some candies that resemble cigarettes might make younger kids think smoking is a good idea. "Like those Popeye Candies," she points out. "They look like cigarettes and maybe kids see the candy and the cigarettes and think, 'Oh, I can have these candies, they're good, and I bet those cigarettes are good too!'"

Meenakshi realizes the negative influence this can have on kids. "It's a way of advertising," she says. "I also see ads in the magazines a lot. If I go through *People* magazine, I usually see one or two cigarette ads." Cigarette advertisements like the ones Meenakshi sees in magazines are a big problem because all they do is try to convince people to smoke. "With the advertising, they try to make you think smoking's cool or feels good," she explains. But she knows that's not true. "There are lots of poisonous chemicals in cigarettes. Smoking is bad for the environment, for you, and for the people around you," she says. A cigarette ad might try to make you think smoking is cool, but Meenakshi points out that, "It's just trying to get you to buy cigarettes, maybe by showing famous people smoking." A celebrity who smokes isn't so cool to Meenakshi. "Why would you idolize someone who's killing themselves?" she asks. "What's the point of sucking in the poisonous stuff that goes into cigarettes? You're slowly killing yourself!"

 In Meenakshi's own words …

Looks Can Be More Than Just Deceiving; Deadly Even

You're watching your favorite show on TV, and then those annoying ads come on. One of them has flashy colors, parodies of celebrities running toward a nightclub trying to get something. At the nightclub, a platinum-gold platter is holding the usual cigarette packet. Let me repeat that: a cigarette packet?! You've got to be kidding.

This may seem like all those other essays you've heard of: "Don't Smoke" "It Hurts Your Game" or "Shaquille O'Neal doesn't do it, why should you?" but you're wrong. This essay includes the dark side of smoking, but from a different viewpoint. We're going behind the scenes of … smoking advertising. There are a lot of questions that are asked about why smoking manufacturers show ads about smoking. The main question that is being focused on throughout this essay is, "Why advertise something that can hurt you?"

Mind Games

There are a few things you need to know about smoking, and that is being aware of cigarette manufacturers' "mind games." If you go into a gas station, you will sometimes see cigarette displays overhanging the candy aisle. It kind of lures you closer to that odd overhanging display. You might even want to try a cigarette. If you like it, you'll buy more and more. Soon, if you keep it up, the hospital might even become your new home. After the hospital comes a very sad place. Cigarette manufacturers *want* you to buy more. Hopefully, you know how to think for yourself and will *not* (notice the key word "not") try (or start) smoking! I can guarantee you smoking will make you sick!

The way manufacturers get you to buy their product is to make it seem cool, the new craze, everybody's doing it. Although it's not always as it seems. Cigarettes have many chemicals in them that harm you and your health. "Why do those cigarette manufacturers sell their deadly product?" you ask. That is because it is very addictive. Cigarettes are addictive. Without a doubt, some people will chain smoke (smoking one cigarette after another, almost nonstop) and yes, you guessed it, buy more! Your parents must have told you, "The only person who can care for you is yourself," "You're on your own in the real world, because no one else will care for you as much as you need it." It's true; your health does not concern the cigarette companies, only your money does. There are scientists who do research on cigarettes and find ways to make the consumers buy more. In other words, they make cigarettes *more* addictive so the money keeps rolling in.

Reeling in the Line

First of all, this is not about fish. Second of all, this is another thing you need to know about ... enticing the customers, or "reeling in the line." You are probably thinking, "What the heck does that mean?" Enticing the consumer means trying to get people to buy your products. This is what cigarette companies are famous for. Sometimes, when you see people smoking, doing drugs, or driving on a race track, you might get enticed to do it. Cigarette companies want to entice younger consumers to try smoking. That way, they can make money off the younger people longer.

A way of enticing consumers is to make it look like their product is not a bad thing. To do that, you would use commercials, advertisements, or anything that promotes your product. Sometimes new features will be added to spark interest. If it's a toy or something, the company will probably add a new feature, like a trip to Pluto, or something, to entice customers.

Now do you realize smoking is wrong? "Tobacco companies are making a killing off you" (AADAC, 2006). So listen to people when they tell you not to smoke. They could just be right about something and save your life and the lives of others. Smoking kills an average of 300 people each day where I live, even as we speak. "No cigarettes, no regrets" (AADAC, 2006) would be a good motto to live by. It might remind you of the consequences of smoking. As the title of this essay says: "Looks Can Be More Than Just Deceiving; Deadly Even."

DID YOU KNOW?

Tobacco companies tailor their ads to the audience that they think is watching. In women's magazines, ads show beautiful women smoking. In adventure magazines the models are fit and active. Billboards are designed for each neighborhood based on the age, salary, and cultural background of the people who live there.[3]

INSTANT HISTORY FACTS

- For a long time, cigarettes have been marketed to men in a way that conveys images of strength and sexiness. In the 1950s, Philip Morris invented a character called the Marlboro Man, a tough cowboy used to advertise their filtered cigarettes. In 1995, one of the actors who played the Marlboro Man, David McLean, died of lung cancer. His widow sued Philip Morris arguing that her husband regularly smoked as many as five packs of cigarettes a day during Marlboro photo shoots and TV commercials. That's a cigarette every five minutes during a 40-hour work week.[4]

- During the first half of the 19th century, women who smoked in public were seen as crass and unladylike. Smoking became popular during women's liberation in the 1920s and 1930s, when women across the western world were fighting for the right to vote and work the same jobs as men. Cigarette companies used this opportunity to advertise cigarettes to women as symbols of equality and strength. Smoking became a symbol of this equality, and women and girls started smoking outside their homes. After WWII, women were targeted by ads that focused on appearance. Big cigarette companies told women that smoking was sophisticated, stylish, feminine, and attractive to men. Cigarette brands such as Virginia Slims told women that smoking would make them thin. The Virginia Slims brand was introduced in 1968. By 1974, the number of 12-year-old girls smoking had increased by 110%.[5]

- Today, the false image of smoking as beautiful and cool is everywhere. Cigarette brands targeting young women suggest that smoking can give you self-confidence, freedom, and independence. In 2007, the brand Camel No. 9 was criticized for trying to appeal to young women by using fashionable hot pink and black packaging and by putting ads in major fashion magazines. Even the name of the cigarettes, Camel No. 9, sounds more like a perfume or a pop song than a product that causes cancer.[6] It's important to remember that a cigarette is just an object that tobacco companies want you to buy. The effects of smoking aren't beautiful or sexy.

Julian Amorelli, 14

Tobacco companies have always used advertising as a way to make people buy their products, and Julian knows that tobacco ads often try to show cigarettes in a positive way. Since tobacco companies are more worried about making money than about the health of smokers, Julian says that these ads only show one side of smoking, and that this side usually doesn't include the consequences. One of Julian's parents smokes, so he has seen how hard it is to quit. Nicotine addiction is something that tobacco companies don't always mention in their ads, and getting hooked on cigarettes causes smokers to have lots of regrets. Julian doesn't regret not lighting up – he wouldn't be able to play soccer, hockey, or swim as well if he smoked. Always having a cigarette in his hand would also keep him from drawing, which is something else that he enjoys.

FAST FACTS

Marlboro and Camel aim more advertisements at young people than any other brands. They target youth through teen magazines, movies, and TV channels. So far, their advertising works: Marlboro and Camel are the most popular brands among young smokers and are also the most recognizable.[7]

Although Julian believes that most people know when they are being targeted by cigarette ads, he thinks that parents and teachers need to become anti-smoking role models for children. He has noticed how tobacco companies try to attract kids by using cartoon characters in their ads and thinks that kids need to be taught about the risks of smoking so that they don't believe everything that they see in magazines, commercials, or on billboards. Julian says that since kids are affected most by what they see in their everyday lives, the image of people smoking cigarettes in advertising and at home sends the message that smoking is okay. Some kids might think that smoking will make them cool or popular, but Julian wants everyone to know that being cool is really about making your own choices instead of doing what tobacco ads say.

 In Julian's own words ...

Many companies use smoking in their advertisements. They reveal cigarettes in many movies and magazines, and on television, and even billboards. The viewers are being persuaded every day by smoking ads. The ads make it seem like it is a great thing to start. They say this is not bad for you, that it's actually good, but they're lying. They're just doing it for the money. These companies know the consequences of smoking and the effects on people when they inhale the nicotine. They have no concern for the well-being of the people – they're just selling a product that will make their company rich. Once people try smoking, they are addicted to it – they are eager for more and more – and that's what the companies see, and they immediately attack the first chance they get.

It is not entirely the fault of cigarette companies that youth are persuaded to smoke. People smoking on the street or on TV have an impact on young viewers who do not know the serious consequences it may bring. The majority are put in a situation and are being provoked by their surroundings. Some parents take the time to explain and inform their children of what they're getting into, others don't care and might be smokers themselves. Children (young teens) are also being persuaded into smoking by their friends. To be part of the clique you have to maintain and follow what's popular within that group. I think that's how most teens started smoking.

Most smokers regret ever starting. They say that smoking prevents them from living to their full capacity in every aspect of their lives: walking, breathing, tasting, smelling. Smokers are being cheated out of a healthier lifestyle, and they are creating barriers for themselves that will prevent them from living to their fullest potentials.

Everyone has freedom of choice, and I think that companies choose to continue making cigarettes, even knowing that this is killing and destroying people's lives, because they care far too much about their profits. So they leave it to people to make their own choices, and there aren't enough people higher up in power who will accept to lose profits in order to stop cigarettes and step forward and take responsibility to completely remove the tobacco industry. They no longer advertise cigarettes on TV or bulletin boards, but they are still sold everywhere. I hope this will eventually become illegal, just like drugs, since we all will be affected in some way or another, seeing people we love get consumed and destroyed by smoking. We have enough pollution in the air that we all breathe; no one should have the right to directly intake something so deadly. To have it banned completely is a step in the right direction.

So be in control of your choices and don't make others choose for you.

ACTIVIST MOMENTS

Did you know that Florida's anti-smoking campaign uses money that they won in a lawsuit against the tobacco industry? In 1997, the tobacco industry had to pay Florida $13 billion, and $200 million of this goes toward reducing teen smoking. The best part is that this campaign is run entirely by teens. They've created their own anti-smoking brand called Truth©, which includes TV, radio, and print ads about the myths of cigarettes. Six months after Truth went public, more then 90 percent of Florida teens knew of at least one aspect of their ad campaign. Their campaign even won awards for its anti-smoking advertising.[8]

FAST FACTS

Tobacco ads are now taken out of school library editions of *Time*, *Newsweek*, *People*, and *Sports Illustrated* magazines.[9] Some magazines are now available in tobacco-free editions to subscribers who want them. Contact your favorite magazines and ask if they have tobacco-free editions, and if they don't, ask "Why not?"[10]

EMPTY POCKETS

Darren Low, 11

What would you buy if you won the lottery? For Darren Low, that is an easy question to answer. "A Ferrari," he exclaims. "A red one!" Although he might not be winning the lottery anytime soon, Darren still wants to save up so he can buy his own car some day. That is one of the reasons why he will never start smoking. He doesn't want to waste his money – or his health – on cigarettes. "I'd rather save the cash for a car or something," he says.

Darren doesn't understand why *anyone* would waste their money on cigarettes. "There are so many chemicals in cigarettes. It's not good for you. It's a waste of money," he says. Buying a pack of cigarettes every day can really add up. Darren explains that "by the time a smoker is thirty years old, he or she can spend maybe $25,000 on cigarettes!" Darren won't be spending any of his hard-earned money on cigarettes. He'd prefer to spend that $25,000 he could save on fun things: "I'd rather have money for a car or vacation. Not cigarettes."

If smoking is such a harmful habit, why do people still do it? "I think some people smoke because they are looking to other people and they think it's cool," says Darren. But as far as Darren is concerned, there is nothing cool about smoking, and there is no good reason why a person should ever start. "I don't know anybody who smokes," he says, "but if I did, I would tell them about how you'll get cancer and stuff, and I'd tell them how much money it will cost."

Smoking is a bad habit that hurts your body *and* your wallet. The people at big tobacco companies who want you to buy cigarettes are not thinking about your health. "The cigarette companies just want your money," Darren agrees. They definitely won't be getting any of his money. "I don't want to smoke. I would rather play hockey and videogames with my friends, and watch TV," he says. "Why would I spend money on cigarettes?" he exclaims, "It's a waste!" When it comes to choosing between a long, healthy life and wasting money on cigarettes that will only make you sick, the smart choice is obvious to Darren. Smoking is just not a good idea. Plus, if he decided to smoke, he would never have enough money to buy that shiny red Ferrari!

 In Darren's own words …

Did you know that smoking causes hardening of the arteries leading to premature risk of heart disease? It can also give you frequent colds, chronic bronchitis, or gastric ulcers. It will also increase your heart and blood pressure. You can get mouth cancer, larynx cancer, pharynx cancer, esophagus cancer, lung cancer, pancreas cancer, cervix cancer, uterus cancer, and bladder cancer. It may diminish or extinguish your sense of smell and taste. You can get emphysema, heart disease, or have a stroke. Another risk is premature face wrinkles.

So would you smoke? I won't. I want to live longer. You should see how many ingredients they put in one cigarette. I would not want to have frequent colds, smoker's cough, chronic bronchitis, gastric ulcers, mouth cancer, larynx cancer, pharynx cancer, esophagus cancer, uterus cancer, bladder cancer, emphysema, heart disease, or strokes. So why be dumb and smoke when it causes all of this? I wouldn't do it. Don't smoke, be smart.

Did you know that if you start smoking at age 13 and stopped at age 30, you would waste approximately $20,000 - $25,000 on cigarettes in just 17 years? You could buy lots of things with that money, like a nice TV, video games, bikes, computers, cars, food, iPod nanos, iPod videos, laptops, pianos, CD players, guitars, diamonds, or cameras.

Source: http://www.heartandstroke.ca

DID YOU KNOW?

Being a smoker now makes it harder to find work. In the United States there are 6,000 employers that won't hire smokers. The list includes a sheriff's department in California, a community college in Michigan, a fire department in Oklahoma[1], and the Union Pacific Railroad. Some companies even test their employees monthly to make sure they are smoke-free, and then charge a fee if the employees are found to be smokers. Hiring smokers costs companies money in health benefits and sick leave. But even if you ignore the fact that smokers are more likely to get sick, it has been found that smokers take an average of seven or eight more sick days than nonsmokers.[2]

INSTANT HISTORY FACTS

In the 1600s, tobacco was a popular crop because it could be farmed on a small scale and didn't require much money to start. But it did need a lot of labor. By 1700 in Maryland and Virginia, black slaves made up one third of the workers in the tobacco fields. Unlike their white servant counterparts, black slaves were usually forbidden to move up the ranks or purchase land of their own.[3]

ACTIVIST MOMENTS

In Fredericksburg, Virginia, the Campaign for Tobacco-Free Kids tried to convince the US National Slavery Museum to return a $200,000 donation from a tobacco company. Matthew Myers, the campaign's president, argued that it wasn't right to build the museum with the help of money from the tobacco industry.[4]

INSTANT HISTORY FACTS

Today, child labor in tobacco fields and cigarette factories is common in many countries. In India, many families sell their children to tobacco companies in order to pay medical bills or to support themselves. A child worker can be bought for $25 - $50 (US). The children work for years, sometimes for their entire lives, rolling cigarettes for very low wages.

US Customs banned the importation of bidis (small hand-rolled cigarettes) in 1999 after a *60 Minutes* report exposed child labor in bidi production by a company in India called Mangalore Ganesh. In the United States, it is illegal to import goods made as a result of child labor.[5]

SMOKING STATS

- About 15 billion cigarettes are sold daily — that's 10 million cigarettes every minute![6]
- Philip Morris tobacco factories make between 8,000 and 12,000 cigarettes every minute.[7]
- In 2006, Altria (the company that owns Philip Morris) made $66,734 million by selling tobacco products.[8]
- While the tobacco industry is raking in the profits, smoking costs everyone else huge amounts of money. Smoking-related illnesses, such as cancer, cost the US more then 150 billion dollars a year in medicine, doctor bills, and emergency care.[9]

FAST FACTS

It costs approximately $8 (US) for a pack of cigarettes. Someone who smoked a pack a day for one year would spend almost $3,000 on cigarettes in that year. That's the cost of over 300 movie tickets or a family vacation.[10]

Victoria Falcon, 14

As a tobacco youth advocate for her school district, Victoria was able to speak to assembly members and senators about tobacco during her state's "lobby day." Sometimes lobby days are organized by an advocacy group for a particular cause and sometimes they are open to any issue. Lobby days are a great way to show your local government that you care about an important issue. Victoria wanted to show support for a bill that would tax cigarettes more heavily, which means smokers would pay more when they bought cigarettes. The students who attended the lobby day hoped the increased cigarette prices would discourage kids and adults from smoking as much and hoped that the move would prevent people from picking up the habit at all. Victoria's motivation behind supporting this bill was to make cigarettes very costly so that people wouldn't be inclined to empty their pockets, only to fill up their lungs with poisonous smoke.

Cigarettes are an issue close to home for Victoria. She tries hard to decrease smoking among her family members and classmates, and in her whole state through straightforward presentations of the facts. You can learn more about these facts and which issues are being debated in your area by contacting your local government official.

In Victoria's own words ...

In my family, I have relatives who smoke cigarettes. Smoking has been a factor in my maternal grandmother's health. My uncle and my grandfather on my mother's side are both smokers. My grandfather stopped smoking permanently awhile ago. His reason to stop was because his doctor told him that if he continued, he would die. My uncle, on the contrary, still smokes regularly and he doesn't seem to mind the proven consequences of smoking. Since I am a tobacco youth advocate for the SFUSD (San Francisco Unified School District), I have tried advocating the clearly defined dangers of smoking to my uncle. However, sometimes even though it's sad, some people won't listen until permanent damage to the body has occurred.

Last spring, I attended a California state lobby day. There, students along with me spoke with assembly members and senators about bills that we wanted them to pass next Election Day. I spoke with assembly woman Patty Berg. I was advocating on the bill that would add a tax to cigarettes. The tax unfortunately didn't pass. As a result, people are still dying of smoking disease. Smoking may have been a factor in some women making heart disease rise on charts. Smoking may seem "cool" to young adults, but don't be fooled or taken in by peer pressure, because you will later suffer.

As a tobacco youth advocate, I have learned the true information about tobacco. In my school, I have done presentations that show data on tobacco to the sixth and seventh grade classes. Hopefully, the students that listened to my presentation will not smoke later on in their life. If local stores stopped selling tobacco products, our beautiful country would be healthier and our healthy hearts would beat in response.

DID YOU KNOW?

Cigarettes don't just cost smokers the price of a pack. Smoking empties their pockets in other ways as well. For example:

- Smokers pay more for health and house insurance.

- Smoke stains on car upholstery lower the worth of smokers' cars.

- Smokers have to dry clean their clothes more frequently to get rid of the smell.

- Smokers spend more money on mints and gum to hide bad breath. They also spend money to whiten their teeth. These seem like small purchases, but they add up.[11]

FAST FACTS

In Bangladesh, the poorest families are twice as likely to smoke as the wealthiest families. The average male cigarette smoker in the country spends more than twice as much money on cigarettes as he does on clothing, housing, health, and education combined. If money was spent on food instead of cigarettes in Bangladesh, about 10.5 million people wouldn't be malnourished and 350 fewer children would die of hunger daily.[12]

In some countries, such as China and Pakistan, 20 cigarettes cost as much as half a day's worth of food. For the cost of a pack of Marlboro cigarettes, you could buy a dozen coconuts in Papua New Guinea or a dozen eggs in Panama.[13]

ACTIVIST MOMENTS

Tyler Ward is the president of Education Bringing Youth Tobacco Truths (E-BUTT) and a student at the University of Toronto. In 2006, he helped empty tobacco companies' pockets by convincing the university to sell the tobacco stock that it owned. Owning stock in tobacco companies meant that whenever these companies made money, the value of the stock the university owned would go up. So, every time the companies sold packs of cigarettes, the university made money. As a result of Ward's encouragement, the university sold approximately $10.5 million worth of tobacco industry stock and banned future tobacco investments by the school. The University of Toronto was the first Canadian university to make this change, but schools such as Harvard, Stanford, and Johns Hopkins have also decided to give up their tobacco investments.[14]

THE PLANET

Madison Whitaker, 10

Madison, known as Maddie to her friends and family, cares about the planet and is well aware that smoking hurts more than just people. She really likes photography, especially taking pictures of nature, and she sometimes worries that the pollution caused by smoking could kill the plants and animals she loves. She says that smokers pollute the earth when they blow cigarette smoke into the air, which makes it the earth's problem too. She has also seen smokers throw their cigarette butts on the ground once they're finished, and thinks that people should be more careful when it comes to littering.

Maddie not only takes care of the planet's health by recycling, but also keeps herself healthy and active with soccer and tae kwon do. Maddie would never try smoking because she knows that it is bad for your health, and she worries about the health of smokers in her family. She thinks that it's important to let people close to you know how you feel about cigarettes, and to talk to those you love about quitting.

 In Madison's own words ...

Why Shouldn't *I* Smoke?

Why shouldn't I smoke? If you're one of those kids who always wonders about this question, just think to yourself, is it *really* healthy to let smoke in yourself, throughout your whole body?

Smoking is seriously dangerous! It can lead to heart disease, cancer, breathing problems, a stroke, and can increase your risk of getting diabetes. Smoking can also change your personal appearance by causing wrinkles, staining your teeth, etc.

People might think cigarettes are cool along with the people who smoke them. They're wrong! Smoking is not cool and there is nothing good about smoking. If your friends smoke and tell you to, don't! *Never* give into peer pressure, no matter what. If your friends threaten you by telling you to smoke or else they won't be your friend, they're not your friend at all! Also, it might be the other way around. What I mean by that is you might have a boyfriend, girlfriend, or friend who doesn't want you to smoke. That's a good thing.

Smoking doesn't just hurt people, it hurts the planet. When people smoke, gas gets in the air and spreads. It then pollutes the air. People who smoke also litter. When they're done with a cigarette, they will throw it on the ground and step on it to burn it out. Unless they use an ashtray, it's littering. Plus, about 50% or more of the time, people smoke outside their house, where there is no ashtray.

If you have a family member that smokes, I know how you feel. You worry that if they don't quit, they could become seriously ill. If you feel that way, sit down and have a talk with them. Maybe they'll think about quitting. And remember, don't just *quit* smoking, never *start*!

FAST FACTS

- Over half of all littered items in the world are cigarette butts.[1] That's about 4.3 trillion cigarette butts littered every year.[2]

- Almost one in three cigarette butts are littered instead of disposed of properly. The US litters over 250 billion cigarette butts a year. Australian smokers litter over 7 billion cigarette butts a year. Smokers in the province of New South Whales, Australia, alone litter enough butts each year to fill seven Olympic swimming pools.[3]

- Cigarette butts aren't the only things littered by smokers – cigarette packaging, lighters, and matches are commonly littered items as well. It takes a lot of hard work and money to clean up this ugly mess, but it won't go away on its own. A cigarette butt can take up to 12 years to break down because the filter is made of cellulose acetate, a plastic that is slow to disintegrate.[4]

Nicholas Williams, 13

One of the reasons Nick feels strongly about clearing the air of cigarette smoke is because he has asthma. If he's exposed to secondhand smoke in public, he finds it difficult to breath. Nick also cares about smoking's effects on the environment and worries about the chemicals that cigarettes are putting into the air. When he sees his neighbors throw cigarette butts on the ground it makes him worry about the litter it causes, and he fears that animals might eat the cigarette stubs and get sick. He knows that this type of littering could even start a fire. Nick feels that it's important for everyone to hear about the many specific dangers of smoking, which is why he's speaking out.

 In Nick's own words …

Smoking Fears and Feelings

Many people may think long and hard about the future, and some of them think of their family.

Smoking can take a family member when no one expects it, and many have to face the facts and realize it's just going to happen. You may fear that smokers in your own family will go to far lengths to get cigarettes for their addiction and you will have to watch them slowly fade away from you and from their life. They will smoke while you watch them suffer. This could dramatically alter your life and more if you're young.

You shouldn't only be concerned about the smoker's health, but also be concerned about the environment. What will happen to the environment?

The smoke that the smoker gives off goes into the air. People near the smoker inhale secondhand smoke, which is just as bad as smoking the cigarette itself. I don't think that the people that try to stay away from smoking want to inhale secondhand smoke. Secondhand smoke in the air can cause people to develop asthma and other illnesses.

Smoke wandering through the air isn't the best thing for anyone or anything. Over time materials around the smoke-filled air may absorb the smoke to make it smell horrible. Not only smoke comes from the cigarette, but ash could fall off the cigarette and could make a mess and possibly start a fire.

Most likely there will be a slip up and something bad will happen. A smoker could fall asleep with a cigarette burning. The cigarette will burn something and a fire will get started. Fires could make the smoker lose all of his or her stuff and that would make smoking and stupidity responsible for the smoker becoming homeless.

DID YOU KNOW?

The cigarettes and cigarette packages so often littered on beaches and coastlines are eaten by fish, whales, birds, and other marine animals. These creatures mistake the trash for food and swallow hazardous chemicals that may make it hard for them to digest everything they eat.[5] Albatross birds have been seen feeding their chicks cigarette lighters because they resemble pumice (a rock that they eat to help digestion). The chicks then die from eating the cigarette lighters.[6]

INSTANT HISTORY FACTS

- Named after a real baby black bear that was found alone, abandoned, and scared after a devastating wildfire in New Mexico, Smokey Bear became a symbol of wildfire safety in 1944. The first Smokey Bear poster warning people to be careful with cigarettes in order to prevent forest fires appeared in 1953.[7]

- One of the world's worst forest fires (which took place in China in 1987) was caused by a cigarette. It killed 300 people and destroyed the homes of 5,000 others. The fire, called the "Great Black Dragon Fire," ravaged 1.3 million hectares ($5,019^{m2}$) of land.[8] That's an area larger than the entire state of Hawaii.

- In 2004, the state of New York became the first in the world to require that the ignition propensity of cigarettes be reduced.[9] This means that cigarettes must be made of materials that are less likely to start fires on upholstered furniture, mattresses, and bedding. Since 2005, Health Canada has also monitored cigarettes that are made in or imported into Canada to make sure that the cigarettes measure up to the new Cigarette Ignition Propensity Regulations.[10] In 2009, the UK will only sell new cigarettes that stop burning within two minutes of being extinguished, in order to help prevent fires caused by cigarettes.[11] However, these cigarettes are far from being "fire safe" – smokers will still need to be careful.

- Several studies released in 2004 concluded that smoking causes an incredible amount of pollution. One study showed that the air in a smoky bar was 2.5 times more polluted than the air on a major highway or a busy city street.[12] Another study showed that cigarette smoke creates 10 times more air pollution than car exhaust.[13]

- In 2006, California became the first state to declare secondhand smoke a toxic air pollutant equal to diesel exhaust and the chemicals arsenic and benzene. Officials decided that the pollution caused by tobacco had to be recognized because the rising rates of breast cancer, heart disease, lung cancer, and premature births can all be linked to secondhand smoke.[14]

DID YOU KNOW?

- Just the way that tobacco is grown and how tobacco products are manufactured harms the environment. The tobacco plant can get diseases very easily, so tobacco growers use huge amounts of pesticides, herbicides, and fertilizers to help the plant grow. But the chemicals in pesticides and fertilizers are **toxic** to humans, animals, and the environment. The chemicals can spread to whole communities through drinking water, other crops, and animals, because the chemicals get into the streams, rivers, and food chains (fish drink the water, other animals eat the fish, and humans eat the animals and the fish). These chemicals, such as methyl bromide, also deplete the ozone layer.[15] And because tobacco sucks up nutrients from the soil around it, tobacco makes it more difficult to grow other crops that we need, such as beans, peas, and rice.[16]

- The tobacco farmers themselves can get sick from growing tobacco because of the chemicals in it. They can get abdominal pains and feel dizzy, weak, and nauseated. It can also change their blood pressure and heart rates.[17]

- After tobacco is harvested, it is **cured** to preserve it for storage, transport, and processing. About 12.5 million acres of forest (that's the size of more than 10 Grand Canyons) are destroyed each year to provide enough trees to cure tobacco. It takes the wood from one whole tree to cure two weeks worth of tobacco for the average smoker.[18] In many developing countries, trees are also cut down to build curing barns and to fuel the curing process.

FAST FACTS

Every year, tobacco farming cuts down a forest the size of New York and Los Angeles combined.[19] Cigarette manufacturing machines use 3.7 miles (6 km) of paper every hour.[20] Tobacco products are not only wrapped in paper – they're sold in packages, and advertised on posters. So even more trees are used. It all adds up.

DID YOU KNOW?

When tobacco products are manufactured into cigarettes, cigars, and smokeless tobacco, billions of kilograms of waste are produced. In one year, the global tobacco industry produces over 5 billion lbs (about 2.3 billion kg) of manufacturing waste and 460 million lbs (209 million kg) of chemical waste.[21] That's the same weight in manufacturing waste as over 300,000 large male elephants, and the same weight in chemical waste as about 30,000 large male elephants, every single year.

ACTIVIST MOMENTS

International Coastal Cleanup Day began when a member of The Ocean Conservancy organized a beach cleanup in 1986. Since then, 91 countries have participated in the annual cleanup. Over 6 million volunteers from around the globe have made a huge difference. They have removed over 100 million pounds of marine litter (litter floating on the water's surface or down on the ocean floor). What they have found is shocking – one out of every three items in the water and on the shores that they picked up was a cigarette butt and/or a part of cigarette packaging.[22]

You can help to organize cleanups in your own area too. Three kids who were disgusted by the litter that they saw on different beaches across America started "No Butts About It" to help clear the earth of cigarette litter. They help clean up beaches and parks, and ask places like college campuses to provide cigarette disposal bins and put up their posters (which help to make smokers aware of the problems with cigarette litter as well as the solutions). People from all over the world have been involved with their campaign. They have also started a petition to require cigarette manufacturers to print "Please Dispose of Butts Properly" messages on every cigarette package. No Butts About It also encourages others to make their own posters or bumper stickers to help smokers break their dirty littering habits.[23]

Now that you've heard why people like you have chosen not to start smoking, follow the steps below to make your own commitment to stay smoke-free.

1. *Grab a pen* and a piece of paper. First, write *I, [insert your name], pledge not to smoke.*

2. *Write* down the main reason(s) why you don't smoke and why you never will.

3. *Think* about what you will say if someone ever offers you a cigarette, and how you feel when you see movies and advertisements that feature tobacco. Write all of these reactions down in your pledge – they may be helpful reminders someday.

4. *Decide* how you will help clear the air for good. How can you spread the word that it's time to make cigarettes history?

5. *Sign* your name at the bottom of your pledge and write the date next to it. Ask your parents to be witnesses and to sign the pledge as well.

6. *Ask* your family and friends to make their own pledges not to smoke. By asking the people you care about to really consider their health and the harmful effects of cigarettes, you're already making a huge change. Talk to your parents about the things you can all do to make sure your household stays smoke-free. Talk to your friends about how you can support each other in your commitments to make sure cigarettes never become a part of your lives. Brainstorm ideas together and promise to watch out for each other.

7. *Display* the pledge in your room so that you can always remember exactly why you choose not to smoke.

8. *Stay true* to your promise to lead a smoke-free life. By doing so, you will help protect yourself as well as everyone around you.

9. *Breathe* freely and...

10. *Enjoy* the clear air!

ENDNOTES

Chapter 1:

1   U.S. Dept. of Health, Education, and Welfare, "Smoking and Health: Report of the Advisory Committee to the Surgeon General of the Public Health Service," Surgeon General's Advisory Committee on Smoking and Health, *Public Health Service Publication* 1103 (1964).

2   U.S. Dept. of Health and Human Services, "New Surgeon General's Report Expands List of Diseases Caused by Smoking," press release, May 27, 2004.

3   Jordan Goodman, ed., "Timeline" in *Tobacco in History and Culture: An Encyclopedia, Vol. 1, xv.* (Detroit: Scribner, 2005).

4   Ibid.

5   Reuters, "Canada's Cigarette Package Warnings to be Part of Exhibit," *The Globe and Mail*, October 8, 2005.

6   Philip Michael Jeffery, "Trade Practices (Consumer Product Information Standards) Regulations 2004," *Statutory Rules 2004* 264, no. 19 (August 2004), http://www.smoke-free.ca/warnings/laws/australia.pdf.

7   Conseil des Ministres, "Plan Fédéral de lutte contre le tabagisme," *Belgique Portail Fédéral,* http://www.belgium.be/eportal/application?languageParameter=fr&pageid=contentPage&docId=33182.

8   Brazilian News Release, "Cigarette Packs Will Display Stronger Images," October 28, 2003, http://www.anvisa.gov.br/eng/informs/news/281003.htm.

9   Chilean Government Press Release, "Chile Gets a New Tobacco Law," August 14, 2006, http://www.chilean-government.cl/index.php?option=com_content&task=view&id=1051.

10 Jordan Information Center, "Graphic Health Warnings to be Included on Cigarette Packets Next Year," March 31, 2005, http://www.smoke-free.ca/warnings/laws/Jordan.mht

11 Honorable Damien O'Connor, "Graphic Warnings for Cigarette Packets," New Zealand government press release, February 11, 2006.

12 Singapore Minister of Health, "Smoking (Control of Advertisements and Sale of Tobacco) Act (Chapter 309)," *Smoking (Control of Advertisements and Sale of Tobacco) (Labelling) Regulations 2003*, July 28, 2003.

13 Départment fédéral de l'intérieur, "Révision de l'ordonnance sur le tabac: mise en vigueur par le Conseil federal," communiqué de press, Octobre 27, 2004.

14 Government of Thailand Public Relations Dept., "Tighter Tobacco Control Regulations," press release, March 18, 2005.

15 Republica Bolivariana de Venezuala Ministerio de Salud y Desarrollo Social, "Nuevas Advertencias Sanitarias en las Cajetillas de Cigarrillos," March 15, 2004.

16 For information on these international laws and for images, please see: Physicians for a Smoke-Free Canada, "Picture Based Cigarette Health Warnings Legislation and Regulations," http://www.smoke-free.ca/warnings/countries%20and%20laws.htm.

17 David Hammond et al., "Text and Graphic Warnings on Cigarette Packages: Findings from the International Tobacco Control Four Country Study," *America Journal of Preventive Medicine* 33, no. 3 (2007).

18 "Graphic Warnings on Cigarette Packages Effective: Study," *Canada AM*, February 6, 2007.

19 M. O'Hegarty et al., "Young adults' perceptions of cigarette warning labels in the United States and Canada," *Preventing Chronic Disease* (April 2007), http://www.cdc.gov/pcd/issues/2007/apr/06_0024.htm.

20 Tobacco-Free Kids, "Smoking's Immediate Effects on the Body," factsheet, http://www.tobaccofreekids.org/research/factsheets/pdf/0264.pdf

21 John M. Broder, "Cigarette Maker Concedes Smoking Can Cause Cancer," *New York Times*, Mar 21, 1997, A1.

22 Ibid.

23 Elizabeth Olson, "U.S. Lengthens the List of Diseases Linked to Smoking," *New York Times*, May 28, 2004.

24 U.S. Dept. of Health and Human Services, "The Health Consequences of Involuntary Exposure to Tobacco Smoke: A Report of the Surgeon General," (Atlanta, GA: U.S. Dept. of Health and Human Services, Centers for Disease Control and Prevention, Coordinating Center for Health Promotion, National Center for Chronic Disease Prevention and Health Promotion, Office on Smoking and Health, 2006).

25 Cancer Research UK, "Smoking and Cancer: What's in a cigarette?" November 2004, http://info.cancerresearchuk.org/healthyliving/smokingandtobacco/whatsinacigarette/.

26 National Cancer Institute (NCI), "The Truth About "Light" Cigarettes," factsheet, August 17, 2004, http://www.cancer.gov/cancertopics/factsheet/Tobacco/light-cigarettes.

27 World Health Organization (WHO), "An International Treaty of Tobacco Control," August 13, 2003, http://www.who.int/features/2003/08/en/.

28   Elizabeth Olson, "U.S. Lengthens the List of Diseases Linked to Smoking," *New York Times*, May 28, 2004.

29   WHO, *World Health Report 1999*

Chapter 2

1   J.G. Johnson et al., "Smoking May Lead to Anxiety Disorders in Adolescents and Young Adults," *JAMA* 284, no. 18 (2000): 2348-2351.

2   L.D. Johnston et al., "Decline in Daily Smoking By Younger Teens Has Ended," national press release, *University of Michigan News Service*, December 21, 2006.

3   Haissam Dahan, DMD., e-mail message to Lauren Clark, March 19, 2007.

4   Eric Nagourney, "Fertility: Nicotine Changes Sperm, and Not for the Better," *New York Times*, October 25, 2005.

5   Centers for Disease Control and Prevention (CDC), "Chronology of Significant Developments Related to Smoking and Health," http://www.ritobaccocontrolnet.com/chrncdc.html.

6   Campaign for Tobacco-Free Kids, "Kick Butts Day: Activities," 2007, http://kickbuttsday.org/activities/activities.html.

7   "Students Work to Kick Butts: Empty footwear symbolizes deaths caused by smoking," The Patriot Ledger, April 6, 2006.

8   Christopher Hope, "New Attack on Smokers Raises Age Limit to 18," *Telegraph.co.uk,* January 2, 2007, http://www.telegraph.co.uk/health/main.jhtml?xml=/health/2007/01/02/nsmoke01.xml.

9   "Cigarette-Buying Age Rise Backed," *BBC News*, January 1, 2007, http://news.bbc.co.uk/2/hi/uk_news/6222785.stm.

10   Canadian Council for Tobacco Control (CCTC), "Summary Analysis of Canadian Laws," February 6, 2007, http://www.cctc.ca/cctc/EN/lawandtobacco/analysis.

11   Campaign for Tobacco-Free Kids, "Where Do Youth Smokers Get Their Cigarettes?" factsheet, 2004, http://www.tobaccofreekids.org/research/factsheets/pdf/0073.pdf.

12   CCTC, "Summary Analysis" (see chap. 2, n. 10).

13   Canadian Cancer Society (CCS), "Youth Tobacco Possession Laws," September 2001, http://www.cancer.ca/vgn/images/portal/cit_776/0/49/72971528cw_youthtobaccopossesionlaws_en.pdf.

14   Ibid.

15   "For Lent, Church Joins War Against Smoking," *The Indian Catholic*, March 12, 2007, http://www.theindiancatholic.com/newsread.asp?nid=6607.

16   Campaign for Tobacco Free Kids, "Smoking and Other Drug Use," factsheet, January 3, 2002, http://tobaccofreekids.org/research/factsheets/pdf/0106.pdf; Center on Addiction and Substance Abuses, "Cigarettes, Alcohol, Marijuana: Gateways to Illicit Drug Use," Columbia University report, October 1994.

Chapter 3

1   Australian Government Department of Health and Ageing, "Young People and Smoking: The Fact File," 2005, http://www.health.gov.au/internet/wcms/publishing.nsf/Content/health-pubhlth-strateg-drugs-tobacco-young-people.htm.

2   U.S. Dept. of Health and Human Services, "Reducing Tobacco Use: A Report of the Surgeon General," (Atlanta, GA: U.S. Department of Health and Human Services, Centers for Disease Control and Prevention, National Center for Chronic Disease Prevention and Health Promotion, Office on Smoking and Health, 2000).

3   Associated Press, "Airlines Report No Big Problems in First Week of Smoking Curbs," *New York Times*, April 28, 1988.

4   Michael Landauer, "Q & A with Anti-Smoking Crusader Patty Young," *Dallas Morning News*, March 4, 2007.

5   U.S. Dept. of Health, "The Health Consequences" (see chap. 1, n. 24).

6   Health Canada, "Canadian Tobacco Use Monitoring Survey," 2004, http://www.hc-sc.gc.ca/hl-vs/tobac-tabac/research-recherche/stat/ctums-esutc/index_e.html.

7   U.S. Dept. of Health, Education and Welfare, "Smoking and Health: A Report of the Surgeon General," (Rockville: U.S. Department of Health, Education and Welfare, Public Health Service, Office of the Assistant Secretary for Health, Office on Smoking and Health, 1979).

8   WHO, "Regulation Urgently Needed to Control Growing List of Deadly Tobacco Products," press release, May 30, 2006.

ENDNOTES

9   Health Canada, "Canadian Tobacco" (see chap. 3, n. 6).

10 U.S. Dept of Health, "The Health Consequences" (see chap. 1, n. 24).

11 Pam Belluck, "Maine City Bans Smoking in Cars Carrying Children," *New York Times*, January 19, 2007.

12 B.C. Singer et al., "Gas-Phase Organics in Environmental Tobacco Smoke," *Environmental Science & Technology* 36, (2002): 846-853.

13 E.R. Bertone, L.A. Snyder and A.S. Moore, "Environmental Tobacco Smoke and Risk of Malignant Lymphoma in Pet Cats," *American Journal of Epidemiology* 156, (2002): 268-273; J.S. Reif, D. Bruns and K.S. Lower, "Cancer of the Nasal Cavity and Paranasal Sinuses and Exposure to Environmental Tobacco Smoke in Pet Dogs," *American Journal of Epidemiology* 147 (1998): 488-492.

Chapter 4

1   Action on Smoking and Health (ASH), "What's in a Cigarette. Factsheet no. 12," November 2006, http://www.ash.org.uk/html/factsheets/html/fact12.html.

2   National Institute on Drug Abuse (NIDA), "NIDA Research Report—Nicotine Addiction," *NIH Pub. No. 01-4342* (Bethesda, MD: August 1998); Michael Siegel, "Unsafe at Any Level," *New York Times*, January 28, 2007.

3   Judith Mackay and Michael Eriksen, "The History of Tobacco," in *The Tobacco Atlas* (Geneva: WHO, 2002), 18-19.

4   American Cancer Society (ACS), "Cigarette Smoking," October 12, 2006, http://www.cancer.org/docroot/PED/content/PED_10_2X_Cigarette_Smoking.asp.

5   Alix M. Freedman, "'Impact Booster'," *Wall Street Journal*, October 18, 1995.

6   Siegel, "Unsafe at Any Level," (see chap. 4, n. 2).

7   Gregory N. Connolly et al., "Trends in Smoke Nicotine Yield and Relationship to Design Characteristics Among Popular U.S. Cigarette Brands," *Harvard School of Public Health Report*, January 2007; Associated Press, "More Nicotine in Cigarettes than 6 Years Ago," January 3, 2007.

8   David Brown, "Nicotine Up Sharply In Many Cigarettes," *The Washington Post*, August 31, 2006; Connolly, "Trends in Smoke" (see chap. 4, n. 7).

9   Health Canada, "It Will Never Happen to Me" factsheet, September 2006, http://www.hc-sc.gc.ca/hl-vs/tobac-tabac/youth-jeunes/scoop-primeur/never-jamais/index_e.html.

10 Loren Stein, "California's Anti-Tobacco Media Campaign," *Caremark Special Report*, January 4, 2007, http://healthresources.caremark.com/topic/casmoking.

11 ASH, "Nicotine and addiction. Factsheet no. 9," March 2007, http://www.ash.org.uk/html/./factsheets/html/fact09.html; I.P Stolerman and M.J. Jarvis, "The Scientific Case that Nicotine is Addictive," *Psychopharmacology* 117 (1995): 2-10.

12 Stein, "California's Anti-Tobacco" (see chap. 4, n.10).

13 Health Canada, "Nicotine Addiction," factsheet, 2005, http://www.hc-sc.gc.ca/hl-vs/tobac-tabac/res/news-nouvelles/fs-if/nicotine_e.html.

14 J.R. DiFranza et al., "Tobacco Acquisition and Cigarette Brand Selection Among Youth," *Tobacco Control* 3 (1994): 334-34; National Campaign for Tobacco-Free Kids, "The Path to Smoking Addiction Starts at Very Young Ages," March 2, 2007, http://www.tobaccofreekids.org/research/factsheets/pdf/0127.pdf.

15 Health Canada, "Nicotine Addiction" (see chap. 4, n.13).

16 Health Canada, "Nicotine," August 2005, http://www.hc-sc.gc.ca/hl-vs/tobac-tabac/body-corps/nicotine/index_e.html.

17 Associated Press, *Tobacco Exec Equates Gummy Bears, Cigarettes*, New York, May 3, 1997.

18 Health Canada, "Smoking and Your Body," November 2006, http://www.hc-sc.gc.ca/hl-vs/tobac-tabac/body-corps/index_e.html.

19 S. Zevin, S.G. Gourlay and N.L. Benowitz, "Clinical Pharmacology Of Nicotine," *Clinics in Dermatology*, 16 (1998): 557-564.

20 Nutt et al., "Development of a Rational Scale to Assess the Harm of Drugs of Potential Misuse," *The Lancet* 369 (2007): 1047-1053.

21 CDC, "You Can Quit Smoking: Nicotine Addiction," http://www.cdc.gov/tobacco/quit_smoking/you_can_quit/nicotine.htm.

ENDNOTES

22 NIDA, "Mind Over Matter: The Brain's Response to Nicotine," *NIH* Pub. No. 00-3858 (Bethesda, MD: 2000).

23 Tara Parker-Pope, *Cigarettes*, (New York, The New Press: 2001).

24 NIDA, "Mind Over Matter" (see chap. 4, n. 22).

25 L. Jacobsen, "Gender-Specific Effects of Prenatal and Adolescent Exposure to Tobacco Smoke on Auditory and Visual Attention," *Neuropsychopharmacology* 21, March 2007.

26 "Smoking Hampers Brain Power in Adolescents," *Pak Tribune*, April 23, 2007, http://www.paktribune.com/news/index.shtml?159625; NIDA, "Brain Power!" *NIH* Pub. No. 01-4575 (Bethesda, MD: 2001). NIDA, "Mind Over Matter" (see chap. 4, n. 22).

27 NCI, "The Truth About 'Light' Cigarettes," factsheet, http://www.cancer.gov/cancertopics/factsheet/Tobacco/light-cigarettes.

28 CDC, "You Can Quit Smoking: Nicotine Addiction," http://www.cdc.gov/tobacco/quit_smoking/you_can_quit/nicotine.htm.

29 Campaign for Tobacco-Free Kids, "Tobacco Harm to Kids," March 2, 2007, http://www.tobaccofreekids.org/research/factsheets/pdf/0077.pdf; A.C. Parrott, "Does Cigarette Smoking Cause Stress?" *American Psychologist* 54 (10): 817-20, 1999.

30 NIDA, "Brain Power!" (see chap. 4, n. 26).

31 CDC, "You Can Quit" (see chap. 4, n. 28).

32 A.C. "Does Cigarette Smoking Cause Stress?" American Psychologist 54, 10 (1999): 817-20.

Chapter 5

1 Sue Anne Pressley, "High School Smokes Out Tobacco Users," *Washington Post,* September 24, 2000.

2 Heart and Stroke Foundation of Saskatchewan and the Canadian Cancer Society, "Tobacco Free Sports," 2004, http://www.tobaccotoolkit.ca/Tobacco_free_sports/Tobacco%20Free%20Sports%20index.htm.

3 National Basketball Association, "Suns Say 'NO!' to Smoking," January, 2006, http://www.nba.com/suns/news/adhs_no_smoking.html.

4 Heart and Stroke, "Tobacco Free" (see chap. 5, n. 2).

5 Alan Blum, "Tobacco in Sport: an Endless Addiction?" *Tobacco Control* 14 (2005): 1-2.

6 Mark Newman, "Play Your (Baseball) Cards Right," MLB.com, May 16, 2006. http://mlb.mlb.com/news/article.jsp?ymd=20060516&content_id=1456133&vkey=news_mlb&fext=.jsp&c_id=mlb.

7 NCI, "Smokeless Tobacco and Cancer," factsheet, http://www.cancer.gov/cancertopics/factsheet/Tobacco/smokeless.

8 TeensHealth, "Smokeless Tobacco," Nemours Foundation, http://www.kidshealth.org/teen/drug_alcohol/tobacco/smokeless.html.

9 U.S. Dept. of Health, "The Health Consequences" (see chap. 1, n. 24).

10 NCI, "Smokeless Tobacco" (see chap. 5, n. 7).

11 U.S. Dept. of Health, "The Health Consequences" (see chap. 1, n. 24).

12 "Rick Bender Talks," *Gasp Magazine* 7, BC Ministry of Health, 2001.

13 Mike Falcon, "Baseball Star Bagwell Snuffs Out Spitting Tobacco," *USA TODAY,* August 1, 2001, http://www.usatoday.com/news/health/spotlight/2001-07-31-bagwell-tobacco.htm.

14 Health Canada, "Smokeless Tobacco," http://www.hc-sc.gc.ca/hl-vs/tobac-tabac/body-corps/smokeless-sansfumee/index_e.html.

15 "The Athlete Project," *Sports Pharmacology*, 2005, http://www.athleteproject.com/member/sportspharm.htm.

16 Reuters, "Smoking Affects Heart of Even the Young and Fit," New York, April 12, 2007.

17 Royal College of Physicians, *Smoking and the Young*, (London: Royal College of Physicians, 2002).

18 Oral Cancer Foundation, "Nicotine and addiction," http://www.oralcancerfoundation.org/tobacco/nicotine_tobacco.htm

19 TeensHealth, "Smoking," 2007, http://www.kidshealth.org/teen/drug_alcohol/tobacco/smoking.html.

20 TeensHealth, "Smokeless Tobacco" (see chap. 5, n. 8).

ENDNOTES

21 Royal College of Physicians, *Smoking and the Young*, (London: Royal College of Physicians, 2002).

22 ActNowBC, "How Does Tobacco Affect Athletic Performance?" Province of British Columbia, 2006, http://www.actnowbc.gov.bc.ca/EN/youth/how_does_tobacco_affect_athletic_performance/.

23 S. Sidney et al, "Cigarette Smoking and Submaximal Exercise Test Duration in a Biracial Population of Young Adults," *Medicine and Science in Sports and Exercise* 25, 8 (1993): 911-916.

24 CDC, "Tobacco-Free Sports Initiatives," February 28, 2007, http://www.cdc.gov/tobacco/youth/educational_materials/sports/index.htm.

25 Little League Online, "Little League Baseball World Series to be Tobacco-Free," August 1, 2006, http://www.little-league.org/media/tobaccofree.asp.

26 TeensHealth, "Smoking" (see chap. 5, n. 19).

27 Silverstein P, "Smoking and Wound Healing," *American Journal of Medicine* 93, 1A (July 1992): 22S-24S; C.I. Adams CI, et al., "Cigarette Smoking and Open Tibial Fractures," *Injury* 32, no. 1 (January 2003): 61-5.

28 Tobacco.org, "Tobacco Timeline," 2003, http://www.tobacco.org/resources/history/Tobacco_History20-1.html.

29 Oral Cancer Foundation, "Sports Figures," 2007, http://www.oralcancerfoundation.org/people/sports_figures.htm.

30 CDC, "Tobacco-Free Sports" (see chap. 5, n. 24).

31 See Thru The Smoke, "Tobacco-Free Teams," 2007, http://www.unfilteredtv.com/act/tobacco_free_teams.php.

32 Pacific Sport, "Tobacco Free Sports," 2006, http://cms.nortia.org/Org/Org26/Content/Main/PSBC/Programs/SportDevelopment/TobaccoFreeSports.asp.

Chapter 6

1   Health Canada, "It Will Never Happen to Me" (see chap. 4, n. 9).

2   Health Canada, "It Will Never Happen to Me" (see chap. 4, n. 9); American Council on Health, "Cigarettes: What the warning label doesn't tell you," press release, 1996.

3   Kadunce DP, et al. "Cigarette Smoking: Risk factor for premature facial wrinkling," *Annals of Internal Medicine* 114, no. 10 (1991): 840–844.

4   Yolanda R. Helfrich, "Effect of Smoking on Aging of Photoprotected Skin," *Archives of Dermatology* 143 (2007): 397-402.

5   Health Canada, "It Will Never Happen to Me" (see chap. 4, n. 9).

6   C.J. O'Doherty and C. MacIntyre, "Palmoplantar Pustulosis and Smoking," *BMJ* 291 (1985): 861-4; L. Naldi et al., "Association of Early-Stage Psoriasis with Smoking and Male Alcohol Consumption," *Archives of Dermatology* 135 (1999): 1479-1484.

7   *Ibid.*

8   *Ibid.*

9   Terry Moloney, dir. *Scene Smoking: Cigarettes, Cinema & the Myth of Cool*, 2001.

10 "Smoking: The Truth Unfiltered," *In The Mix*. PBS. Transcript online: http://www.pbs.org/inthemix/shows/show_smoking.html

11 "Susan Sarandon's Advice on How to Stay Looking Young," Female First.co.uk, October 2004.

12 "Quit Smoking to Save Your Teeth," *BBC News*, July 18, 2005, http://news.bbc.co.uk/1/hi/health/4692531.stm.

13 J.R. Evans et al., "28,000 Cases of Age-Related Macular Degeneration Causing Visual Loss," *British Journal of Ophthalmology* 89 (2005): 550-53.

14 Health Canada, "It Will Never Happen to Me" (see chap. 4, n. 9).

15 P.E. Hysert et al., "'At Face Value,'" *Tobacco Control* 12 (2003): 238.

16 APRIL age progression ,"APRIL Software," http://www.aprilage.com/.

17 Judith Mackay and Michael Eriksen, "Youth," in *The Tobacco Atlas* (Geneva: WHO, 2002), 28-29.

18 Health Canada, "It Will Never Happen to Me" (see chap. 4, n. 9).

19 R.M. Trueb, "Association Between Smoking and Hair Loss," *Dermatology* 206, no. 3 (2003): 189-91.

ENDNOTES

20 Tobacco Research and Intervention Program, "Smoking and Weight," pamphlet, 2007, www.smokefree.gov/pubs/FFree3.pdf.

21 Associated Press, "Smoking Diseases Hitting Women Harder," *Herald Sun*, April 15, 2007, http://www.news.com.au/heraldsun/story/0,,21560205-5005961,00.html.

22 I. Karp et al., "Risk Factors for Tobacco Dependence in Adolescent Smokers," *Tobacco Control* 15 (2006): 199-204; CTV.ca news staff, "Smoking Doesn't Slim Girls; Stunts Boys' Growth," *CTV.ca*, October 24, 2006, http://www.ctv.ca/servlet/ArticleNews/story/CTVNews/20061024/teen_girls_smoking_061924/20061024?hub=TopStories

Chapter 7

1   Reuters UK, "Movie Group Slaps New Restrictions on Smoking," Los Angeles, May 11, 2007.

2   Jim Puzzanghera, "Hollywood Set to Filter On-screen Smoking," *Los Angles Times*, May 11, 2007.

3   Associated Press, "All Roads Lead Back To Church For Hudson," Chicago, February 20, 2007.

4   "Interview: Natalie Portman. Heart to Heart with Natalie Portman," *Barnes&noble.com Interview*, Sept 26, 2000, http://video.barnesandnoble.com/.

5   Ali Gazan, "Obsessed Completely," *YM*, 2005, http://www.ym.com/jsp/stars/inthespotlight/oct2703.jsp.

6   Sandra J. Teel et al., "Lessons Learned from the Broadcast Cigarette Advertising Ban," *Journal of Marketing* 43, no. 1 (Jan 1979): 45-50.

7   J. Sargent et al., "Brand Appearances in Contemporary Cinema Films and Contribution to Global Marketing of Cigarettes," *Lancet* 357, no. 9249 (January 2001): 29-32.

8   P. Magnus, "Superman and the Marlboro Woman," *NY State Journal of Medicine* 85 (1985): 342-343.

9   The Foundation for a Smokefree America, "More Anti-Smoking Issues in Movies and TV," *Tobaccofree.org*, http://www.tobaccofree.org/films.htm.

10 CTV.ca news staff, "Anti-Smoking Activists Target TIFF, Hollywood," *CTV.ca*, September 8, 2006, http://www.ctv.ca/servlet/ArticleNews/story/CTVNews/20060908/smoking_movies_060908/20060908?s_name=tiff2006.

11 C. Mekemson and S.A. Glantz, "How the Tobacco Industry Built its Relationship with Hollywood," *Tobacco Control* 11.1 (2002): i81-i91.

12 Anna M. Adachi-Mejia et al., "Tobacco Brand Appearances in Movies Before and After the Master Settlement Agreement," *JAMA* 293, no. 19 (May 2005): 2341-2342.

13 Smoke Free Movies, "Our Ads," 2002, http://www.smokefreemovies.ucsf.edu/ourads/textonly_superman_var.html.

14 Christopher John Farley, "C'mon, Baby, Light my Fire," *Time*, Jan 27, 1997.Harvard School of Public Health (HSPH), "HSPH Releases Presentations Made to Motion Picture Association of America on the Depiction of Tobacco Smoking in Movies," press release, April 3, 2007, http://www.hsph.harvard.edu/news/press-releases/2007-releases/press04032007.html.

15 Foundation for a Smokefree America, "More Anti-Smoking Issues in Movies and TV" (see chap. 7, n. 9).

16 ACS, "On-Screen Smoking Influences Adolescent Audience," *ACS News Center*, March 9, 2001, http://www.cancer.org/docroot/NWS/content/NWS_2_1x_On_Screen_Smoking_Influences_Adolescent_Audience.asp.

17 P. Raeburn, Associated Press, "Video-Tobacco Ads," New York, January 15, 1990.

18 CTV, "Anti-Smoking" (see chap. 7, n. 10); B. Alamar and S.A. Glantz, "Tobacco Industry Profits From Smoking Images in the Movies," *Pediatrics* 117, no. 4 (April 2006): 1462.

19 American Legacy Foundation and J.D. Sargent et al., "Youth Exposure to Smoking in Movies," *Pediatrics* 116, 5 (2005): 1183-1191.

20 Professor Stan Glantz, University of California at San Francisco, "Study Says Smoking in Movies is Increasing," press release, March 2, 1998.

21 Sargent, "Brand Appearances" (see chap. 7, n. 7).

22 Crystal Ng and Bradley Dakake, "Tobacco At The Movies: Tobacco Use In PG-13 Films," MASSPIRG Education Fund, Boston, http://www.masspirg.org/reports/TobaccoattheMovies.pdf.

23 HSPH, "HSPH Releases" (see chap. 7, n. 15).

24 HSPH, "Presentations to the Motion Picture Association of America (MPAA) on Smoking in the Movies," press release, Hollywood, CA, February 23, 2007, http://www.hsph.harvard.edu/mpaa.

25   Boliek, Brooks. "Most Think Film Smoking Sways Kids," Reuters, Feb 13, 2007.

Chapter 8

1   Cheryl Albright et al., "How Cigarettes Are Advertised in Magazines," *Health Communication* 3, no. 2 (1991): 75-91.

2   "Why Are You Buying Your Food From a Tobacco Company?" *Adbusters*, http://www.adbusters.org/spoofads/food/products/; BBC News staff, "Philip Morris buys Nabisco," *BBC News Online*, June 26, 2000, http://newsvote.bbc.co.uk/2/hi/business/806105.stm.

3   Yael Bloom et al., "Smoke Signs: Patterns of tobacco billboard advertising in a metropolitan region," *Tobacco Control* 9 (2000): 16-23.

4   P.M. Ling and A. Toll, "The Virginia Slims Identity Crisis," *Tobacco Control* 14 (2005): 172-180; D. Kellner, "Reading Images Critically: Toward a postmodern pedagogy," *Journal of Education* 170, no. 3 (1988): 31-52; Steve James, "'Marlboro Man' Widow Wins Round," *Reuters*, Aug 27, 1999.

5   Ling, "Virginia Slims"; CBC News staff, "Tobacco Companies Designed Cigarettes to Addict Women, Study Says," *CBC News*, May 2005, http://www.cbc.ca/health/story/2005/05/30/tobacco050530.html; S.J. Anderson, P.M. Ling and A. Stanton, "Emotions For Sale," *Tobacco Control* 14 (2005): 127-135; J.P. Pierce, L. Lee and E.A. Gilpin, "Smoking Initiation by Adolescent Girls, 1944 through 1988," *JAMA* 271, no. 8 (1994).

6   Stuart Elliot, "A New Camel Brand is Dressed to the Nines," *New York Times*, February 24, 2007; CBC, "Tobacco Companies" (see chap. 8, n. 5); Anderson, "Emotions for Sale" (see chap. 8, n. 5).

7   Carolyn Celebucki et al., "Adolescent Exposure to Cigarette Advertising in Magazines," *Journal of the American Medical Association* 279 (1998): 516-520; CBC, "Tobacco Companies" (see chap. 8, n. 5); Anderson, "Emotions for Sale" (see chap. 8, n. 5);

8   University of Florida, "Artful Truth: Exposing the Smokescreen of Advertising," Florida International University Magazine, Spring 1999.

9   American Library Association, "Tobacco Ads Stripped from School Library Magazine Editions," *Bulletin*, June 24, 2005, http://www.ala.org/ala/alonline/currentnews/newsarchive/2005abc/june2005a/tobaccoads.cfm.

10   Andrew Clark, "On America," *Guardian Unlimited*

Chapter 9

1   T. Gustafson, P. Levin and A. Velenchik, "More Bad News For Smokers?" *Industrial and Labor Relations Review* 50, no. 3 (1997): 493-509.

2   Jennifer Barrett Ozols, "A Job or a Cigarette?" *Newsweek*, February 24, 2005; Nicholas Bakalar, "Study Finds Smokers Take More Sick Leave," *International Herald Tribune*, April 11, 2007.

3   Ira Berlin, *Many Thousands Gone* (Cambridge: Harvard University Press, 1998).

4   Associated Press, "Anti-Smoking Group Demands Slavery Museum Return Tobacco Company Donation," *Fox News*, March 20, 2007.

5   WHO, "Tobacco and Poverty. A Vicious Circle," brochure, 2004, http://www.who.int/tobacco/communications/events/wntd/2004/en/wntd2004_brochure_en.pdf; Scott Pelley, "Tobacco Slaves in India," *CBS News*, August 29, 2000, http://www.cbsnews.com/stories/1999/11/22/60II/main71386.shtml

6   WHO, "Smoking Statistics," May 28, 2002, http://www.wpro.who.int/media_centre/fact_sheets/fs_20020528.htm.

7   Philip Morris Intl., "From Seed to Pack," 2006, http://www.philipmorrisinternational.com/pmintl/pages/eng/ourbus/Factory_tour.asp.

8   Altria Group, Inc., "2006 Atria Annual Report," 2007, http://www.altria.com/investors/02_01_annualreport.asp.

9   WHO, "Smoking Statistics" (see chap. 9, n. 6).

10   Health Canada, "The Real Cost," 2005, http://www.hc-sc.gc.ca/hl-vs/tobac-tabac/youth-jeunes/scoop-primeur/know-savoir/realcost-coutsreels_e.html.

11   Hilary Smith, "The High Cost of Smoking," *MSN Money*, http://articles.moneycentral.msn.com/Insurance/InsureYourHealth/HighCostOfSmoking.aspx?wa=wsignin1.0.

12   D. Efroymson et al., "Hungry For Tobacco: An analysis of the economic impact of tobacco consumption on the poor in Bangladesh," *Tobacco Control* 10 (2001): 212-217.

13   Judith Mackay and Michael Eriksen, "Costs to the Smoker," in *The Tobacco Atlas* (Geneva, WHO, 2002), 42-43.

ENDNOTES

14 Lauren La Rose, "U of T to Sells Off Tobacco Shares: Students," *Toronto Star*, April 9, 2007, http://www.thestar.com/News/article/201121.

Chapter 10

1   R. Curnow and Community Change 2001, "Measuring Environmentally Desirable Behaviour," *Beverage Industry Environment Council Littering Behaviour Study III*, 2001.

2   Australian Local Government Association, "2005 National General Assembly of Local Government," *Business Papers* 2005, http://www.lga.sa.gov.au/webdata/resources/files/ALGA_Notices_of_Motion.pdf.

3   *Ibid.*

4   Victoria Government, "Information for Smokers and the General Public," Sustainability Victoria, April 13, 2007, http://www.sustainability.vic.gov.au/www/html/2362-information-for-smokers-and-the-general-public.asp; K. Register, "Cigarette Butts as Litter – Toxic as well as ugly," *Underwater Naturalist. Bulletin of the American littoral society* 25, no. 2 (August 2000).

5   Register, "Cigarette Butts as Litter" (see chap. 10, n. 4).

6   Hillary Mayell, "Environmental Movement at 40: Is Earth Healthier?" *National Geographic News*, April 19, 2002, http://news.nationalgeographic.com/news/2002/04/0419_020419_rachelcarson.html.

7   "Smokey's Vault," SmokeyBear.com, http://www.smokeybear.com.

8   Judith Mackay and Michael Eriksen, "Costs to the Economy," in *The Tobacco Atlas* (Geneva: WHO, 2002), 40-41.

9   Health Canada, "Regulatory Proposal for Reducing Fire Risks from Cigarettes. A Consultation Paper," Dec 2002, http://www.hc-sc.gc.ca/hl-vs/alt_formats/hecs-sesc/pdf/pubs/tobac-tabac/ripc-cpar/fire-incendie_e.pdf; R.J. O'Connor et al., "Smokers' Reactions to Reduced Ignition Propensity Cigarettes," *Tobacco Control* 15, no. 1 (February 2006): 45-9.

10 Health Canada, "Reduced Ignition Propensity Cigarettes," November 20, 2006, http://www.hc-sc.gc.ca/hl-vs/tobac-tabac/legislation/reg/ignition-alllumage/index_e.html.

11 Denis Campbell. "New 'Fire-Safe' Cigarettes Will Put Themselves Out," *The Observer UK*, May 27, 2007.

12 James Repace, "Respirable Particles and Carcinogens in the Air of Delaware Hospitality Venues Before and After a Smoking Ban," *JOEM* 46, no. 9 (2004): 887-905.

13 G. Invernizzi et al., "Particulate Matter From Tobacco Versus Diesel Car Exhaust," *Tobacco Control*, 13, no. 3 (September 2004): 219-21.

14 Associated Press, "Calif. Declares Secondhand Smoke a Pollutant," *MSNBC News Services*, January 27, 2006, http://www.msnbc.msn.com/id/11048609/.

15 ASH, "Tobacco and the Environment. Fact Sheet no. 22," July 2004, http://www.ash.org.uk/html/factsheets/html/fact22.html; M. Barry, "The Influence of the US Tobacco Industry on the Health, Economy, and Environment of Developing Countries," *New England Journal of Medicine* 324 (1991): 917-9.

16 H.J. Geist, "Global Assessment of Deforestation Related to Tobacco Farming," *Tobacco Control* 8 (1999): 18-28; Geist, *Coping with Changing Environments*, (Neuss, Germany: Ashgate Publications, 1999).

17 WHO, "Tobacco and Poverty" (see chap. 9, n. 5);

18 Dept. of Health, WA, "Tobacco and the Environment," *Oxygen.org.au*, http://www.oxygen.org.au/images/upload/Tobacco%20%20the%20environment.pdf; ASH, "Tobacco and the Environment" (see chap. 10, note 15); Geist, "Global Assessment" (see chap. 10, n. 16).

19 Geist, "Global Assessment" (see chap. 10, n. 16).

20 WWF, "Agriculture and Environment," 2005, http://www.panda.org/about_wwf/what_we_do/policy/agriculture_environment/commodities/tobacco/environmental_impacts/index.cfm.

21 WHO, "Tobacco and Poverty" (see chap. 9, n. 5); T.E. Novotny and F. Zhao, "Consumption and Production Waste: another externality of tobacco use," *Tobacco Control* 8 (1999): 75–80.

22 Robyn Blumner, "Smokers, Keep Your Butts All to Yourselves," *St. Petersburg Times*, April 22, 2007.

23 No Butts About It, http://www.nobuttsaboutit.net/index.html.

RESOURCES

ANTI-TOBACCO ORGANIZATIONS

Campaign for Tobacco Free Kids, www.tobaccofreekids.org
This organization keeps you up to date on the anti-smoking fight around the world. One of the most thorough websites out there!

truth, www.thetruth.com
This website isn't afraid to show the ugly side of tobacco. Read shocking facts, play interactive games, and download anti-smoking videos, posters, and wallpaper.

HEALTH & QUITTING

CANADA:
Health Canada, Youth Zone, www.hc-sc.gc.ca/hl-vs/tobac-tabac/youth-jeunes/index_e.html
Use the calculator to figure out how much money someone could save if he or she quits today.

Canadian Cancer Society
www.cancer.ca/ccs/internet/standard/0,3182,3172_12971__langId-en,00.html
Read about how to keep your life smoke-free, both inside and outside the house, or call the free and confidential Smokers' Helpline to find out how you can help a smoker in your life quit.

US:
American Cancer Society, Tobacco and Cancer, http://www.cancer.org/docroot/PED/PED_10.asp
Every year, on the third Thursday of November, smokers all over the US try to quit smoking. Read 14 creative ways you can help a smoker quit, or encourage them with a "You can do it!" e-card.

American Lung Association, Tobacco Control, www.lungusa.org
Sign a petition to make America smoke-free by 2010, and join Teens Against Tobacco Use (TATU).

ACTIVITIES

World Health Organization, World No Tobacco Day,
http://www.who.int/tobacco/communications/events/wntd/2007/en/index.html
Check out events planned in cities around the world for World No Tobacco Day and add your own event to the list.

US
Kick Butts Day, http://kickbuttsday.org
Find out what's happening for Kick Butts Day in your town! The website also includes the cost, timeline, and a guide for planning your own events.

ENVIRONMENT

Environmental Protection Agency, www.epa.gov/smokefree/publications.html
Learn how secondhand smoke affects the environment as well as the health of your family and pets. Pamphlets and brochures are available in English and Spanish.

US
Keep America Beautiful, Cigarette Litter Prevention Program, http://www.kab.org/aboutus.asp?id=51&rid=76
Find out how to stop cigarette litter in your area and how to start your own litter prevention campaign.

GLOSSARY

Glossary of terms that appear in bold text throughout the book.

Activist: Someone who takes action for or against an issue to create change.

Addiction: See **Addictive**

Addictive: Addictive substances, such as nicotine in tobacco, cause addiction. Addiction is the craving or need to use a habit-forming substance. Without it, the body will experience signs of withdrawal, such as feelings of anxiety, nervousness, irritability, and headaches.

Agoraphobia: A type of anxiety disorder. This fear can keep someone from feeling safe in public places or prevent them from entering public places.

Asthma: A condition where the bronchial tubes in the lungs are irritated and airways to the lungs tighten, causing wheezing, coughing, the production of mucus, and difficulty breathing.

Ban: To stop something from happening by making it illegal.

Big Tobacco: Refers to America's largest tobacco companies, often including but not necessarily limited to the "big three": Philip Morris Inc., R.J. Reynolds Tobacco Co., and British American Tobacco.

Bill: A proposed law or legislation presented for approval to a legislature. In the United States, a bill becomes a law when it is accepted by the **Congress** and the President. If the President vetoes a bill but two-thirds of Congress vote for it, Congress can override the President and pass it.

Blood pressure: When the heart beats, it pumps blood into the arteries. Blood pressure is the measure of the force of the blood against the walls of the arteries. High blood pressure can cause the heart to enlarge, which may cause heart failure. It can also harden the arteries, which can cause heart attacks, strokes, and kidney failures.

Bronchitis: A disease caused by a swelling of the bronchial tubes, which are the main air passages that lead to the lungs. Bronchitis causes regular coughing and the production of mucus. Cigarette smoking is the most common cause of chronic bronchitis.

Cancer: A disease that occurs when cells in the body become abnormal and form groups of abnormal cells called *tumors*. These cells can stay in one part of the body or spread. Cancers are named after the part of the body where they start, and can be found in many areas of the body, including the lungs, throat, lip, breast, prostate, colon, pancreas, bladder, kidney, and skin. Cancer can cause death.

Cancer-causing agents: Also called *carcinogens*, cancer-causing agents are substances that can lead to cancer. All tobacco products contain cancer-causing agents. Secondhand smoke is also considered a cancer-causing agent.

Carbon monoxide: A tasteless, odorless, and poisonous gas found in the exhaust of cars and in tobacco smoke.

Cataracts: A disorder of the eye most often caused by aging and tobacco use. Cataracts form a thick film over the eye that makes vision blurry and can cause blindness.

Censor: To control speech and expression by removing information that is considered objectionable.

Chewing tobacco: A type of **spit tobacco** that is placed inside the cheek in the form of a wad. Users suck and chew on the tobacco, and nicotine is absorbed through the tissues in the mouth and goes into the bloodstream.

Cigar: Tobacco leaves that are dried, fermented, and rolled. Cigars are usually larger than cigarettes but come in many sizes. Cigars are not supposed to be inhaled, but because of the high level of nicotine that they contain, they can create dependence even when the smoke is not inhaled.

Circulation: Blood circulates through the body inside the circulatory system, carrying nutrients and oxygen to cells and removing waste. If the blood is not circulating properly, cells and body tissues do not get enough blood and can die.

Congress: In a congressional system of government (also called a "presidential system"), a congress is the main legislative body (the assembly with the power to adopt laws). In the United States, Congress consists of the Senate and the House of Representatives.

Cured: Tobacco is cured to emphasize its taste and flavor. Curing destroys the chlorophyll in tobacco, which makes the color of the tobacco yellow, converts starch into sugar, and removes the water in tobacco.

Diabetes: A disease in which either the pancreas can't produce enough insulin or the body can't use the insulin the pancreas produces. Insulin is needed to control glucose levels and to help use the energy in carbohydrates.

Dopamine: A chemical messenger in the brain that controls movement, emotional response, and feelings of pleasure and pain. Some drugs, such as nicotine, raise the levels of dopamine that produce feelings of pleasure. This may explain why it is so hard for people to stop smoking.

Dry snuff: See **Snuff**

Emphysema: A lung disease in which the air sacs in the lower lungs lose elasticity, which causes shortness of breath and difficulty exhaling. Smoking is one of the main causes of emphysema.

Exhale: To breathe out.

Filters: Cigarette filters are on the end of the cigarette that is put between the lips. Filters have little holes designed to reduce the amount of smoke, tar, and other particles from being inhaled. However, there are many reasons why filters are not always particularly effective, and smokers may cover the holes with their fingers and lips.

Gallbladder problems: The gallbladder stores and releases bile to help digest fat. Sometimes, bile can form into gallstones, which can be big enough to block the bile duct. If this happens, it can cause severe abdominal pain and the gallbladder may need to be removed.

Gateway (drug): Gateway drugs are believed to lead to the abuse of other drugs.

Generalized anxiety disorder: People with this disorder worry more than most, even when there is nothing to worry about.

Halitosis: The medical term for bad breath. It can be caused by many things, including smoking, poor oral hygiene, and certain foods. The smell comes from a buildup of bacteria in the mouth.

Heart disease: Occurs when the arteries (vessels) that supply blood to the heart muscle become hardened or narrowed. This is caused by the buildup of a fatty substance called plaque. When the blood supply to the heart muscle slows or becomes blocked, a heart attack may occur. Smoking is one of the primary risk factors of heart disease.

Heart dysfunction: A condition where the heart is unable to pump an adequate supply of blood to meet the body's oxygen needs, which may lead to heart failure or a heart attack.

GLOSSARY

Heart rate: Also called *heart beat* or *pulse*, heart rate is the number of heart beats per minute.

High blood pressure: See **Blood pressure**

Immunity: Resistance against illness. Being sick or taking up habits such as smoking can make it more difficult for the body to fight off illness.

Impotence: Also called *erectile dysfunction*, impotence occurs when a male is unable to keep an erection and/or ejaculate.

Larynx: The organ in the throat that contains the vocal cords and is used for speech.

Lawsuit: A dispute that is brought to a court of law in order to hear and settle the matter.

Legal age: The legal age or *age of majority* marks the age that a person can legally buy alcohol and cigarettes, vote, and be tried in court as an adult. People under the age of majority are *minors*.

Lesions: A change in an organ or tissue caused by a disease or injury. Lesions can be caused by many things, including smoking, chewing tobacco, and drinking. They can be cancerous or non-cancerous.

Leukemia: A type of cancer in which the body produces a large number of abnormally shaped blood cells. It usually affects the white blood cells that help the body fight off infections and illnesses.

Lobbying: See **Lobbyist**

Lobbyist: A person who tries to influence an official to take an action or make a decision for a specific cause. Lobbying is the act of working to influence an official.

Lung cancer: A type of cancer in which lumps form in the tissue of the lungs. These lumps or *tumors* can be fatal and can spread through the body. Lung cancer likely develops from the irritation caused by smoking or secondhand smoke.

Lung diseases: Disease where the lungs cannot work properly because airways to the lungs are narrowed or blocked.

Master Settlement Agreement (MSA): In 1998, the five biggest tobacco companies in the United States promised to pay $206 billion dollars to make up for the medical costs of smoking-related diseases and to help reduce smoking. This was called the Master Settlement Agreement. They also promised to ban cartoon characters in advertising, outdoor advertising targeted to youth, youth access to free samples, and to stop sponsoring events with youth audiences.

Moist snuff: See **Snuff tobacco**

Nauseated: To feel the urge to throw up. Nausea may be brought on by many things, including the use of a tobacco product.

Neurons: Neurons carry information through the nervous system.

Nicotine: A poisonous substance found in tobacco and insecticide. Nicotine is a drug in tobacco that makes tobacco addictive.

Oral cancer: Includes cancer of the lip, tongue, cheek, gums, and the floor and roof of the mouth. Tobacco or alcohol use increases the risk of oral cancer. See also: **Cancer**

Panic disorder: A type of anxiety disorder that causes unexpected and intense fear that can last for minutes and even hours.

Pesticide: Substances that destroy and deter pests (insects, weeds, birds, mammals, and fish) from crops or property. Pesticides are often poisonous to humans.

Petition: A written request for a change that is signed by numerous people and submitted to an official organization or person.

Pneumonia: Caused by inflammation of one or both of the lungs from an infection from bacteria or a virus. This happens when germs and irritants, such as tobacco smoke, are breathed in and settle in the tiny air sacs in the lungs. The air sacs then fill with pus and mucus, which keeps the oxygen from reaching the bloodstream as it should.

Possession: See **Youth possession laws**

Respiratory (problems): Respiratory problems can affect the upper respiratory system, which includes the nose, ears, sinuses, and throat, and can cause a runny or stuffy nose, sore throat, coughing, and high fevers. Respiratory problems can also affect the lower respiratory system, which includes the bronchial tubes and the lungs, and can cause difficulty in breathing, coughing with mucus, chest pain, wheezing, and infections such as pneumonia.

Retailers: Retailers buy products in large quantities from manufacturers or importers and sell them in small quantities to the public, usually in a store.

Secondhand smoke: Also known as environmental tobacco smoke (ETS), this includes *sidestream smoke* (the smoke that comes from the end of a lit cigar, cigarette, or pipe), plus *mainstream smoke*, the smoke that the smoker exhales.

Smokeless tobacco: See **Spit tobacco**

Snuff tobacco: A type of spit tobacco. **Moist snuff** is wet and ground up or cut up and **dry snuff** is dry and finely ground to a powder.

Spit Tobacco: Snuff and chewing tobacco are both types of spit tobacco. Spit tobacco is a form of smokeless tobacco that is either chewed or sucked and then spit out. Spit tobacco contains nicotine.

Stroke: Caused by a burst or clot in the blood vessels that carry oxygen and nutrients to the brain. When the blood is no longer supplied to the brain, the surrounding nerve cells in the brain die within minutes and there is a sudden loss of consciousness. Strokes can be fatal.

Tobacco: Found in the leaves of the *Nicotiana tabacum* plant and can be formed into cigarettes and other products. All of the forms of tobacco are addictive and dangerous to the user's health.

Tobacco companies: Companies that grow, ship, market, advertise, and sell cigarettes, cigars, snuff, chewing and pipe tobacco.

Toxin: A poison produced by certain bacteria, plants, or animals that can seriously harm the human body.

Tumor: An abnormal mass of tissue. There are many types of tumors, and treatment for the tumor depends on its type and location. Tumors may be *benign*, meaning that they are non-cancerous, or *malignant*, meaning that the tumor is cancerous.

Vendors: A person or company that sells property, goods, or services for money.

Youth possession laws: Laws that penalize young people for buying or attempting to buy tobacco products, using tobacco products, or having tobacco products in their possession.

Glossary content reviewed by Sharon Taylor, BScN, Smoking Cessation Program Coordinator, McGill University Health Center (MUHC), Montreal Children's Hospital

INDEX